Coping with Pregnancy Loss

loss can leave us with many unanswered questions, and knowing
nd answers is not always clear.

is for you if, like me, you've been affected by any kind of pregnancy
ently or in the past. It provides practical advice and self-care strat-
p you cope during or after loss, alongside ideas that will enable you
:nse of what's happened – including understanding your feelings
s; outlining what you can expect during and after your loss; ways to
lysical and mental health care (if appropriate); and thinking about
member your baby. It's for charities, support groups, therapists, and
professionals who want to provide support and care.

– and cope with loss – in different ways, and this book respects
ls when it comes to getting information and help. You don't have
you are going through your loss alone. In this book you'll find
:ercises, self-help resources, and stories and suggestions from
about how they survived, which should leave you feeling more
l better able to seek additional support if you need it.

Petra Bc n is an Agony Aunt/Advice Columnist, and Social Psychologist
based in East Sussex; working in International Health Research on sex and
relationships issues.

'A deeply useful, practical and sympathetic resource that will be invaluable for anyone affected. It can be difficult to find the right words when it comes to pregnancy loss, but Petra Boynton has done just that.'

Justine Roberts, Founder and CEO of Mumsnet

'Pregnancy loss can be devastating, and for some it's a life-changing experience. It's a time of shock, sadness and grief, but also one of questions and confusion. It's times like this you really need a sympathetic ear, a shoulder to cry on, or someone that can support and guide you through. This book is the companion that everyone needs. Not only is it packed with expert information and advice, Petra's empathy and compassion shine through on every page. From understanding why loss occurs, to how partners can be affected, to getting help and support, this is an invaluable resource.'

Dr Ranj Singh, NHS Doctor and TV Presenter

Coping with
Pregnancy Loss

Petra Boynton

Routledge
Taylor & Francis Group

LONDON AND NEW YORK

First published 2019
by Routledge
2 Park Square, Milton Park, Abingdon, Oxon OX14 4RN

and by Routledge
52 Vanderbilt Avenue, New York, NY 10017

Routledge is an imprint of the Taylor & Francis Group, an informa business

© 2019 Petra Boynton

The right of Petra Boynton to be identified as author of this work has been asserted by her in accordance with sections 77 and 78 of the Copyright, Designs and Patents Act 1988.

British Library Cataloguing-in-Publication Data
A catalogue record for this book is available from the British Library

Library of Congress Cataloging-in-Publication Data
A catalog record has been requested for this book

ISBN: 978-1-138-04772-3 (hbk)
ISBN: 978-1-138-04773-0 (pbk)
ISBN: 978-1-315-17064-0 (ebk)

Typeset in Minion Pro
by Out of House Publishing

Table of
CONTENTS

I nicknamed the baby I lost in my second miscarriage 'bunting'.
Illustrator Sean Longcroft very kindly drew me one and you'll see this
little bird appearing throughout the book. I hope it brings you
reassurance as it does me.

Acknowledgements

To everyone who has shared their stories of pregnancy loss with me – this book would not have been written without your willingness to be so open. I hope it honours your memories and your babies.

Thank you to Sean Longcroft for his patience and kindness in creating the illustrations for this book that represent so many experiences of loss.

I am particularly grateful to Ruth Bender Atik, Lisa Dixon, and Penny Kerry at the Miscarriage Association for allowing me to help with their 'Partners Too' campaign. And to Rob Eagle, Kate Evans, Ruth Howells, and Hilary Jackson for their assistance with that project.

To Verity Sullivan for checking the medical content of this book; Ronete Cohen for insights on therapy and self-care; and Meg-John Barker and Justin Hancock for information about sex and relationships.

To the many charities, NGOs, healthcare practitioners, and therapists who provided ideas and oversight, as well as encouragement to produce a friendly and easy-to-read book that they could recommend to patients and clients.

Many thanks to Catherine MacLellan, Amie Wilson, Jody Day, Margaret McCarthy, Liz Peel, Maria Wolters, and Katie Seik, for being so generous with their time and knowledge. And to Julie Voce, Debbie Epstein, Leah Boynton-Collett, Adam Reisman, Bisi Alimi, Marcia Rigby, Alice Sagwidza-Tembe, Jo Brodie, David Waldock, Caroline Tradewell, Joab ToSaasire, Meena Pajunen, Marie Dixon, Helen Barker, Trevor Mathers, Bruce Maybloom, Ceri Butler, Tania Carson and especially Clare Fisher for their feedback on design and content.

To Eleanor Reedy for her hard work in seeing this book grow from a little idea to a supportive and beautiful resource. And to all who helped with production and promotion – Rob Wilkinson, Abigail Stanley, Alex Howard, Clare Owen, Tom Eden, Daniel Freeman, Liz Mallett.

Special wishes go to Will, Adam, and Aiden for their love and understanding. To Aayush and Lekdhen with pride. And to Jo O'Regan-Jane for good company and cake.

This book is for Anna Raeburn – who is wonderful and wise.

1. Welcome

Whoever you are, however you chose this book, I hope you find it consoling, supportive, and practically useful.

You may have picked this book if you or your partner are miscarrying at the moment; or have experienced pregnancy loss recently or in the past. Alternatively you may be a friend or relative of someone who has had a loss and want to know how best to support a loved one. Or you could be a therapist or healthcare provider looking to understand miscarriage and stillbirth better, or seeking resources to recommend for those in your care.

Pregnancy loss is far reaching and can affect us whether we are young or older parents; whether we are single or in a relationship; regardless if we already have children; however we conceived; whatever our gender or sexuality; whether we had one loss or many; recently or many years ago.

This book was written to help you:

- make more sense of what is going on and understand how you are feeling;
- locate and navigate healthcare, therapy, and support services;
- feel less alone;
- strengthen your relationship (if you are in one);
- feel more in control;
- be assertive when dealing with friends, family, work colleagues, and others in your community; and
- remember, and move on after loss in ways that suit you best.

How to use this book

To ensure you are able to find the right information to suit your needs I have used subtitles and section headings within chapters so that you can anticipate what is going to be talked about. You can skip what is not relevant, or return to any topics that are important but you may not currently feel up to reading.

A guide to what's in the remainder of the book can be found in the at-a-glance guide below.

Chapter 1: Welcome	Outlines what to expect from the text, and ideas for getting the best from the book.
Chapter 2: Facts, figures, and symptoms of pregnancy loss	How often loss happens, symptoms, planning for a loss, what to do in an emergency.
Chapter 3: How to manage your loss	Treatment options for early and late miscarriage, stillbirth, ectopic pregnancy, molar pregnancy, and stillbirth. Communicating your loss with other people.
Chapter 4: What to expect from healthcare	Describes health practitioners who you may encounter and care standards.
Chapter 5: Your emotions during and after pregnancy loss	Outlines the diverse range of reactions you may experience and how to deal with them.
Chapter 6: Making sense of what has happened	Common reasons people give for their losses, and where to get help if other people are unsupportive.
Chapter 7: The needs and feelings of partners	Identifying how partners may react, why they can be left out, and where to get help.
Chapter 8: Taking care of you	Suggestions for looking out for your own wellbeing.

Every chapter contains exercises, quotes from people describing their losses, further reading materials, and recommended websites. You may wish to read the book alone, or share all or part of it with your partner, friends, relatives or your doctor. And you may get more from the book by making notes, and reflecting on key sections that are meaningful.

THE 10 CS OF PREGNANCY LOSS

Some things are CONSISTENT – pregnancy loss is a common, and an inevitable part of pregnancy for many of us.

Some aspects are CHANGEABLE – the circumstances relating to your loss(es); your attitude towards your loss(es) and that of others around you; the kind of care you may need or receive; and how the COMMUNITY and CULTURE in which you live responds to pregnancy loss.

Some things are CONTRADICTORY – you may not be sure what is going on or know what to do for the best; have many CONFUSING and bewildering reactions to your loss; or be given lots of CONFLICTING advice.

Some parts of pregnancy loss you can COPE with, while others may be a CRISIS.

There is no one-size-fits-all approach to pregnancy loss. It is not a COMPETITION.

Why did I write Coping With Pregnancy Loss?

I've worked as an Agony Aunt (advice columnist) for the past two decades and get many messages from people affected by pregnancy loss. At the same time I have been lecturing and researching within International Health Research, supporting individuals, organisations, and charities to provide better miscarriage care. In 2014 I carried out research for the Miscarriage Association (funded by a Beacon Bursary from University College London's Public Engagement Unit) learning how loss affected partners. I have also had three miscarriages.

Disclaimer

This book is not a replacement for medical care, and there is information in Chapter 2 on where you can get help and what to do in an emergency. Other people have also written excellent texts about many of the topics covered in this book, including clinical information, and I have linked to a selection you might want to use if you wish to read more.

Chapter 2
(pp. 12–13)

Links to websites and social media provided in this book are correct at time of going to press, and will be kept updated at www.copingwithpregnancyloss.com.

BEFORE YOU GO FURTHER...

As you are reading this book it may help you to occasionally check in with yourself and ask:

> How am I feeling?
>
> What help do I need right now?
>
> Is there anything I am particularly troubled by? If so, who can help me and what can I do about it?
>
> How am I going to care for myself today?

Follow the butterfly

Butterflies have long been used as a symbol of pregnancy loss. In this book you'll see butterflies in the margins directing you to sources of help elsewhere in the text.

2. *Facts, Figures,*
AND SYMPTOMS OF PREGNANCY LOSS

After my miscarriages I kept seeing the same figures mentioned. You may have noticed them too. An estimated 1 in 5 pregnancies (20%) end in baby loss, with 85% of losses happening in the first 12 weeks of pregnancy.

Knowing this can be reassuring. It helps you realize you are not alone and that other people have gone through pregnancy loss too. It reminds us that while it may be upsetting, early miscarriage is very common. And it may be comforting to note while 1 in 5 pregnancies does not last, 4 in 5 do, encouraging many of us to try again to get pregnant.

Numbers are not always useful, however. Knowing how often miscarriages occur makes little difference to living through and after loss. It may be particularly troubling if you have had multiple losses, or if you feel any loss needs to have more humanity to it than just a statistic. And just because pregnancy loss is common, it can still come as a shock or disappointment.

PREGNANCY LOSS IN NUMBERS

1 in 5 pregnancies (20%) end in miscarriage

12,000 pregnancies (1 in every 80–90) per year are ectopic.[1]

Around 1 in 600 pregnancies is a molar pregnancy.[2]

In 2015 there were 2.6 million recorded stillbirths worldwide. The vast majority (98%) in low-income countries.[3]

Recurrent miscarriages affect 1 in 100 women in the UK (in low-income countries this figure is higher).[4]

After two consecutive miscarriages you have a 91% chance of conceiving again. This reduces to 20% if you have had seven or more miscarriages.[5]

Miscarriage rates in women double after age 40 and triple after age 45,[6] and if partners or sperm donors are aged 40 or older.[7]

Other factors that can increase miscarriage risk include previous pregnancy loss(es); assisted conception; regular or high rates of drinking alcohol; and being underweight.[8]

Having a previous live birth, healthy lifestyles, having sex, and nausea during early pregnancy are all linked to a reduced rate of pregnancy loss (though they cannot guarantee no loss will occur).[9]

Having some context to pregnancy loss can be useful. But it may leave you with further questions or worries. Which in turn can increase feelings of guilt, fear or anxiety (see Chapter 5).

Chapter 5
(pp. 53–57)

> 66 *I went searching for information online and found lots of data but I got the most reassuring answers talking to my doctor and reading information leaflets on a pregnancy loss charity's website.* 99 **Ginny**

MISCARRIAGE SYMPTOMS

Physical symptoms of loss can include

- Pain in your stomach or lower back
- Period-like pains/cramps (may be more intense than usual period)
- Passing clots or what looks like tissue. (If you are able to save this, put it in a container and keep refrigerated until you see your doctor)
- Vaginal bleeding: needing to use a new sanitary pad every hour or less
- Either not developing pregnancy symptoms (e.g. morning sickness); or existing symptoms reducing or stopping (e.g. breast tenderness may reduce, or in a later pregnancy loss you cannot feel baby moving)

Psychological symptoms of loss can include

- Crying, anxiety, fear, numbness, confusion, disbelief, sorrow, desperation, rage (see Chapter 5)

Chapter 5
(pp. 53–57)

If you are unsure of your symptoms but are worried you might be miscarrying call your doctor, Early Pregnancy Unit (if available), or local hospital to find out what services are available to you. It is always better to check.

Some losses can be very painful and you may bleed heavily (see section later in this chapter, 'In an Emergency'). But sometimes there are few or no symptoms prior to losing a pregnancy. It can also be the case that some pregnancies have very few symptoms, or people experience cramping or light bleeding during their pregnancy (particularly in the early weeks), but go on to carry their baby to term.

    " I was so excited about being pregnant, it was a shock to see the blood in my panties. " **Jerusha**

    " I had this overwhelming sense of dread. It didn't feel right. I called the doctor and a loss was later confirmed. " **Abi**

    " I'd had a miscarriage before so I immediately knew when I was having another. " **Michele**

If you have previously had a miscarriage, ectopic pregnancy or stillbirth symptoms of loss may be familiar to you. You may feel able to manage because you know what to expect and do, but equally another loss may leave you so upset that you are unable to focus.

Different Kinds of Pregnancy Loss

TYPE OF LOSS	WHAT HAPPENS?
Threatened miscarriage	where you have some warning signs (bleeding or cramping), but the pregnancy continues.
Early miscarriage	a loss before 12 weeks.
Late miscarriage	a loss after 12 weeks and before 24 weeks.
Complete miscarriage	where there is no remaining pregnancy tissue left in the womb.
Incomplete miscarriage	a loss where not all tissue comes out of your womb and you may need medical help to remove it.

Losses can occur in the first, second or third trimester, and during or immediately after birth. Definitions using weeks here may vary slightly across different countries and states depending on how pregnancy loss is categorized.

You may experience only one loss; recurrent loss (three or more miscarriages consecutively); losses in subsequent pregnancies after having children, or in between pregnancies; or one or more of any of these types of losses.

Pregnancy loss can happen anytime, anywhere

While miscarriage and stillbirth can happen at home, or be managed in hospital (see Chapters 3–4) there is no restriction on where a loss may occur. You could be out shopping, on holiday, at work, or travelling when you experience your loss. There is also no guarantee about timings, meaning you could have a loss on significant days – a birthday, during a festive period, or another meaningful occasion – or just an average day. Your loss may begin while you are awake, or when asleep. It may be something that is very messy, noticeable

Missed/delayed miscarriage	where you have no indication the pregnancy has ended and your loss is discovered later, usually during a scan.
Chemical pregnancy	a loss that happens just after implantation where an ultrasound would not be able to identify the pregnancy, but a pregnancy test shows positive.
Molar pregnancy	a molar pregnancy (hydatidiform mole) happens when a fertilized egg is not viable (meaning won't develop into a baby) but implants in the womb and grows into a mass that looks like grapes.
Ectopic pregnancy	where your baby develops outside the womb (usually in the Fallopian tube).
Stillbirth	where a pregnancy loss happens after 24 weeks.

and painful; that might require medical attention; or be something you can self-manage. It may be very quick, or take time.

Ways to manage your loss

You may decide to wait and see what happens – and let your loss happen without additional interventions; or you may opt to have the pregnancy loss managed with medical care. Sometimes you do not have time to make decisions (for example if you miscarry while at home, or experience heavy bleeding and require emergency hospital care).

Planning for loss

If you are experiencing loss at the moment or worry you may experience this in the future, creating a coping plan may help you feel more secure.

MY COPING PLAN

- Who will I call right away (partner, friend, family member; doctor, ambulance, Early Pregnancy Unit)? Make sure you store emergency numbers in your phone and have them written on a piece of paper to carry with you.
- Where do I need to go (your doctor, Accident and Emergency (the ER), Early Pregnancy Unit)?
- Do I need anyone to help (someone to look after existing children, pets, or provide work cover)?
- Who else needs to know what is going on (work, existing children's school etc.)? Ensure you have contact numbers or emails to hand. You may want to nominate someone to take charge of doing this for you. You do not have to give details unless you want to; 'an emergency' or 'a health issue' will suffice.
- Do I have the supplies I need (a change of clothes, overnight bag, nightwear, sanitary towels, toiletries)?
- How do I want to manage my miscarriage? (See Chapter 3 for options.)
- Who do I want to talk about my miscarriage with (friends, family etc.)? Is there anyone I do NOT want to be told?
- Where else can I get help if I need it? (For example, charities or support groups – see Sources of support.)

Chapter 3
(pp. 21–27)

Sources of
support
(pp. 145–147)

In an emergency

You should call your GP/family doctor or go to Accident and Emergency (the ER) if you are experiencing the following physical or psychological symptoms:

- Bleeding or spotting
- Stomach pain and cramping
- If you are being sick, have diarrhoea (or both)
- Feeling dizzy, light-headed, disconnected from reality, or if you faint

- If you have a stabbing pain in the tip of your shoulder (which may indicate ectopic pregnancy)
- If you have anxiety or depression, or a pre-existing mental health condition that may worsen due to your loss
- If you are feeling suicidal or have attempted to end your life (you can also always use the organisations listed below if you need help).

SUICIDE AND CRISIS CARE CHARITIES

Samaritans www.samaritans.org

National Suicide Prevention Lifeline (US)
https://suicide preventionlifeline.org

Lifeline (Australia) www.lifeline.org.au

Suicide Prevention (Canada) www.suicideprevention.ca

CALM (suicide prevention service for men)
www.the calmzone.net

The Trevor Project (for young LGBTQ people)
www.thetrevorproject.org

You can find links to other suicide prevention organizations via Befrienders Worldwide www.befrienders.org

FURTHER HELP

Miscarriage: What Every Woman Needs to Know (2018) Lesley Regan. Orion Spring.

When a Baby Dies: The Experience of Miscarriage, Stillbirth and Neonatal Death (Revised Ed) (2001) Nancy Kohner and Alix Henley. Routledge.

Notes

1 'Ectopic Pregnancy', *NHS Choices*, www.nhs.uk/conditions/ectopic-pregnancy, last accessed 26 November 2017.

2 'Molar Pregnancy', *NHS Choices*, www.nhs.uk/conditions/molar-pregnancy, last accessed 7 December 2017.

3 'Stillbirths', *World Health* Organization, www.who.int/maternal_child_adolescent/epidemiology/stillbirth/en, last accessed 26 November 2017.

4 Royal College of Obstetricians and Gynaeccologists (2012) *Recurrent and late miscarriage: Tests and treatment of couples.*

5 M. Sugiura-Ogasawara, Y. Ozaki, T. Kitaori, *et al.* (2009) 'Live birth rate according to maternal age and previous number of recurrent miscarriages', *American Journal of Reproductive Immunology* 62, 314–319.

6 A. Nybo Andersen, J. Wohlfahrt, P. Christens, J. Olsen, and M. Melbye (2000) 'Maternal age and fetal loss: population based register linkage study', *British Medical Journal* 320, 1708–1712.

7 K. Kleinhaus, M. Perrin, Y. Friedlander, *et al.* (2006) 'Paternal age and spontaneous abortion', *Obstetrics & Gynecology* 108, 2, 369–377.

8 N. Maconochie, P. Doyle, S. Prior, and R. Simmons (2007) 'Risk factors for first trimester miscarriage: Results from a UK-population-based case-control study', *BJOG – an International Journal of Obstetrics* 114 (2007), 2, 170–186; Department of Health (UK) (2016) *Health Risks from Alcohol*; D. Jurkovic, C. Overton, and R. Bender-Atik (2013) 'Diagnosis and management of first trimester miscarriage', *British Medical Journal*, 346, 34–37.

9 N. Maconochie, P. Doyle, S. Prior, and R. Simmons (2007) 'Risk factors for first trimester miscarriage: Results from a UK-population-based case-control study', *BJOG – an International Journal of Obstetrics* 114, 2, 170–186; S. N. Hinkle, S. L. Mumford, K. L. Grantz, *et al.* (2016) 'Association of Nausea and vomiting during pregnancy with pregnancy loss: A secondary analysis of a randomized clinical trial', *JAMA Internal Medicine* 176, 11, 1621–1627.

3. *How to*
MANAGE YOUR LOSS

Just as there are different ways to experience pregnancy loss, there are also a number of choices available to managing miscarriage. This chapter introduces the different options that may be available to you; explains what they involve; and outlines how you may react to them emotionally.

What am I going to do?

While having a description of what choices are available can help you make decisions, you may be worried about which one is right for you. Talking to your doctor, staff at the hospital or Early Pregnancy Unit (if available), or hearing from others in support groups about their experiences may be reassuring (see Sources of support on where to find these). I felt very strongly during my second miscarriage that I wanted to manage it myself without any medical interventions, but during the course of that miscarriage I changed my mind and opted for surgical management after reading more about it online.

Sources of support (pp. 145–147)

MY PREGNANCY LOSS PLAN

- Where you want to manage your loss (home or hospital)
- If you want expectant, medical or surgical management
- What pain relief you may prefer
- Who you would like to be with you and/or notified in an emergency
- If you wish to speak to a hospital chaplain or specifically do not want this
- If you have any other pre-existing mental or physical health conditions healthcare staff should be aware of
- If you have experienced losses before
- If you have particular needs regarding accessibility, interpreters, or other accommodations (if you are autistic this might also include specific support needed, or clear explanations and instructions about what to expect)
- Other useful instructions for healthcare staff to help you cope while receiving care, such as *I have had a bad experience with a previous pregnancy loss, please reassure me at all stages* or *I would prefer not to have any details about what is happening*
- What you want to happen after your loss (post mortem/autopsy, funeral or other arrangements for the hospital to manage remains).

For some individuals, cultures, and communities, the involvement of family is vital when making important decisions and you may be comforted by having other people around you who share in your grief and support you during and after your loss. That may extend to faith leaders or elders. Alternatively, you may prefer to make decisions by yourself, or with your partner (if you are in a relationship). Remember, while partners, friends, and family may have opinions, ultimately you need to pick something that makes you feel able to cope with the pregnancy loss and is the best option to keep you physically and psychologically healthy.

COMMON QUESTIONS AND WORRIES
YOU MAY HAVE REGARDING TREATMENT CHOICES

You can ask healthcare professionals, charities and support groups ...

- Will it hurt?
- How long will it take?
- What can I expect to happen?
- Will this loss stop me getting pregnant again?
- What are the risks involved?
- Could I get an infection?
- I still feel pregnant, I don't want to do anything in case I'm not really having a miscarriage!
- I don't want to lose my baby, I want to keep them with me.
- I'm scared of a general anaesthetic!
- I hate the thought of carrying a dead baby inside me, can you help me with this?
- I just want this over with! Please can you tell me the best thing to do?
- Can my partner stay with me?
- Can my family be involved (or, alternatively, kept away)?
- How many hospital visits will I need to make?
- Do I need to stay in hospital, and if so, how long for?

Consent

Depending on how you manage your pregnancy loss you may be asked to sign a consent form (if you are having medical or surgical management) to indicate if you wish to organize cremation or burial or if you want the hospital to arrange this, and if you want any pathology tests or a post mortem/autopsy. The doctor should clearly explain every step of the consent process, checking with you that you have understood. If you are not sure what they have told you or the implications of any choices given, it is a good idea to ask for clarification or more time to think about it and talk to others (including family or faith leaders) if appropriate.

How will I know if I am experiencing pregnancy loss?

You may well have a good idea because you have pain, bleeding or have passed clots or what you can recognize as your baby. Alternatively you may have either had no pregnancy symptoms, or still have pregnancy symptoms in which case the pregnancy ending will be discovered by *urine tests*, *blood tests*, and *ultrasound scans* which may include a transvaginal exam (where a small probe is inserted into the vagina in order to see inside the womb) and/ or a scan carried out externally over your stomach; or in the case of ectopic pregnancy with a *laparoscopy* (surgery carried out under general anaesthetic where a camera is inserted through your tummy so doctors can see what is going on with your reproductive organs). You may need more than one blood test or scan before a clear diagnosis can be made, which may involve more than one visit to hospital.

*❝ I decided I wanted to let things happen naturally,
and I lost the pregnancy at home where I felt safe although
very sad. ❞* Joelle

**THINGS THAT MAY HELP YOU
COPE DURING AND IMMEDIATELY AFTER LOSS**

- Over-the-counter painkillers
- Hot water bottle
- Lying in bed or sitting on loo, walking or moving your hips
- Deep breathing (as the pain may feel like what you expected labour to be like so can be upsetting)
- Resting
- More absorbent sanitary towels than you would usually use.
- Having towels available to sit or lie on (if you're worried about blood getting on furniture or bedding)
- Cleaning products (if you, a partner or friend/family member needs to clean up after loss)
- Food and snacks available, with meals cooked for you if you don't feel up to it (ready meals and takeaways may be a useful temporary measure).

If you have an early loss

Chapter 2
(p. 8)

Sources
of support
(pp. 145–147)

Early miscarriage (before 12 weeks) may feel no more painful than a regular period, but it could be closer to labour-like pains that are unexpectedly strong and bleeding that is heaver and goes on for a longer period than anticipated. Whether or not it is physically painful, it may be more difficult to cope with emotionally as you know it is not a 'normal period'. You can speak to your doctor about pain relief, or if you notice worrying symptoms (see Chapter 2), and if you are struggling emotionally – in which case the support groups listed in Sources of support can also help. If you know you are miscarrying you may want to opt for *Natural/Expectant* management of miscarriage where you allow the loss to happen without any other action taken.

An expectant miscarriage may be very quick, but can also take a few weeks and in that time you may not know if your pregnancy has ended – further urine and blood tests and scans will confirm this. You may pass tissue or a complete embryo or fetus and you may want to keep this in a container to show your doctor or have tested (if appropriate). If you are passing large clots, feel faint, are in a lot of pain, and are frightened or distressed, you should call your GP or go to the ER/Accident and Emergency.

❝ I passed tissue when I was on the loo and I flushed by accident. A nurse told me later this happens a lot and wasn't a sign I didn't care or had done anything wrong. ❞ Camila

If you have a missed or incomplete miscarriage (see Chapter 2) you will be given other options including *Medical Management* – using drugs to start or bring forward your loss; or *Surgical Management* – where you have an operation (under local or general anaesthetic) to remove pregnancy tissue.

Chapter 2
(p. 10)

❝ After I learned I was no longer pregnant my doctor offered me some choices. Nothing was happening so after some thought and talking it over with my mum I decided to take drugs. It wasn't an easy choice but once things started I felt like I could accept what had happened. ❞ Iloana

You may also pick these options if you want to end the miscarriage as soon as possible. Some people want the reassurance of hospital care, others are worried about having an anaesthetic and surgical procedure. If you have questions about what will happen and your recovery your doctor can advise.

Medical management

You will take drugs to bring on your labour, after taking a drug that makes your cervix open and your uterus to cramp so you pass your pregnancy. You may be given the medication to insert into your vagina, or take it orally (by mouth). Different healthcare settings have different protocols so in some places you might be offered one drug, in others two. If your pregnancy was between 10–12 weeks this is usually done in hospital, but if you are under 10 weeks pregnant you use the medication at home and miscarry there. Talk to the hospital about your preferences. The medication usually works within two hours, possibly sooner, and the cramps will be stronger than your usual period pains so your hospital may offer pain relief, or provide suggestions to help you cope with any discomfort. Ask for this if it is not offered and you want it. You may want to move around during this time, practise deep breathing; have your partner or a friend or family member rub your back; or lie in bed with a hot water bottle on your stomach or back. You might find it more comfortable to sit on the toilet. You will want to use extra absorbent sanitary towels and possibly put bath towels on your bed or chair to avoid staining. You may be advised to keep any tissue you pass in a container for further testing, or prefer to bury your baby in your garden or other meaningful place. If you have this procedure in hospital they can dispose of remains in a respectful way. Usually this procedure is straightforward, but if

Sources of
support
(pp. 145–147)

the pregnancy is not completely passed you may need to repeat the procedure or opt for surgical management to remove any remaining tissue.

Surgical management

Is also called an ERPC (evacuation of retained products of conception) and you may hear doctors use this term although many people dislike it – *"it sounds overly clinical and disrespectful, it's **my baby**, not 'retained products'"* Mia. Its other name is D&C (dilation and curettage) which you may have heard of. During this procedure, which happens under local or general anaesthetic, your cervix is widened (dilated) and the contents of your uterus removed (via suction). You will not feel this but you may feel sore afterwards and have some bleeding for a few days so will need to use sanitary pads. You can ask for medication prior to the anaesthetic to stop nausea when you come round, and the surgical team will all be aware what your procedure is for. The hospital will dispose of any remains respectfully – or you can ask if you wish to organize a funeral yourself. Depending on when you have the procedure you may go home the same day, or have an overnight stay in hospital. You will need someone to accompany you home and to be with you after surgery to ensure you are physically okay – and you will probably want emotional support too.

Some people continue working through their loss if they manage it naturally, however most require a few days to cope with bleeding, pain, and the psychological reactions to loss. If you have a medical or surgical miscarriage you may need a week or more off work, or longer if you are struggling psychologically. Ask your doctor for a note if you need to be off work, and alert them if your work is liable to be unsympathetic.

Molar pregnancy care

You may miscarry the molar pregnancy naturally, or may need surgical management (see above). After the loss you will need to provide urine samples at home and blood tests at the hospital; both are sent off to specialist centres for testing. If pregnancy hormones continue to rise you may be offered a course of chemotherapy to ensure any remaining cells are destroyed. Depending on where you live you may need to travel to receive this treatment if it is not offered at your local hospital; this can be disruptive, expensive and stressful.

Treating ectopic pregnancy

Depending on how you are doing physically there are several ways an ectopic pregnancy might be managed. These include waiting to see if the ectopic pregnancy ends with no further help, and/or regular checking at the hospital of your physical health, blood tests to check pregnancy hormone levels and ultrasound scans (this is sometimes called *expectant* or *conservative management*). Alternatively, if your pregnancy hormone levels are low and you are physically healthy, you may be offered a drug such as methotrexate that ends the pregnancy developing (*medical management*), during which time you will be montored carefully to check your response to treatment. Or if you are very sick, if there is a live ectopic pregnancy, or your pregnancy hormone levels are very high you will be offered *surgical management* (this may be carried out by keyhole surgery or abdominal surgery).

You may be anxious about future fertility, and the pain and other physical symptoms may be hard to cope with physically and psychologically. You may feel conflicted if you are making sense of potentially being pregnant while having a pregnancy that cannot continue to term and may be highly dangerous if allowed to continue (due to risk of rupture and internal bleeding). Feelings of shock and fear may hit you during or after diagnosis or treatment and you may also have strong and upsetting memories about symptoms. You may be very worried this could happen again (there is a 7–10 per cent change of another ectopic pregnancy, so talk to your doctor or the charities listed in Sources of support if you are anxious.).

Sources of support
(pp. 145–147)

> 66 *It helped me to find out what caused my ectopic pregnancy, by talking to doctors and a charity.* 99 Suki

If you have medical management of ectopic pregnancy you may be fit enough for work within a few days, but surgical management may require a week's recovery (for laparoscopic treatment) or a month to six weeks absence if you had abdominal surgery. It's important to rest and recover afterwards. Talking to your doctor after treatment is important as there are risks to future fertility from an ectopic pregnancy (although this may vary depending on how early the pregnancy was discovered and what treatment you received).

Care for late loss

In a second trimester loss you may have a *natural miscarriage* – where labour-like pains begin and possibly your waters break, followed by delivering your baby. Sometimes if a baby has died you may not know until you have a scan, after which time hospital staff can help induce labour. You can take some time to come to terms with this – *"I wasn't ready to accept the pregnancy was over. I needed some time"* Kirsten; or you may want it to happen as soon as can be arranged – *"She wanted to be induced pretty much immediately"* David.

You should be able to labour in a private room with staff that are appropriately trained to support you throughout. In standard pregnancy books preparing for labour is often presented positively and as something you can be in full control of. But the experience of delivering a baby that has died is very different. You may still wish to prepare for labour by bathing or showering while you are labouring (if not otherwise advised by your midwife or doctor), or using massage oil for lower back massage, focusing on your breathing, walking or moving your hips may help with the pain. However, not everyone wishes to do this or finds it possible if feelings of sadness and panic are present. Your midwife will be able to coach and comfort you, while offering and explaining pain relief options.

Ending a pregnancy with a fetal abnormality

In some cases where a fetal abnormality is discovered you may prefer to end the pregnancy. That may be because you do not wish to cause the baby any further pain, or because psychologically carrying the baby to term is distressing. Much of the care offered in these circumstances is similar to late losses so see elsewhere in this chapter for further information. Deciding to end the pregnancy may be something you feel clearly and strongly needs to happen, or you may want time to make this choice. You can seek advice and information from your doctor, midwife, and support groups such as ARC (Antenatal Results and Choices, www.arc-uk.org).

Chapter 13
(pp. 133–141)

Your doctor and midwife can advise you about what will happen when you end the pregnancy, what pain relief will be offered, how you might want to labour and what your baby may look like on delivery. If you want to have a blessing or other ritual for your baby before or after your termination this should be arranged with the hospital or done at home. You may also wish to create other keepsakes (see Chapter 13). This may be something you involve other people in, or keep strictly private. If you prefer to proceed with the termination with no other ritual or ceremony this is also your choice.

> 66 *I ended my pregnancy at 19 weeks.*
> *My midwife told me baby might move*
> *after delivery but it was too small*
> *and too sick to survive. I opted not to*
> *look. The staff took good care of me*
> *and the baby.* 99 Tiffany

> 66 *She did not want to go through this*
> *so had an anaesthetic. It really helped*
> *her mentally, I don't think she would*
> *have coped otherwise.* 99 Jackson

If your baby is over 21 weeks you will have the choice to be induced so your baby will be born alive but will not survive for long after delivery; or for your baby to be given a drug in the womb to end their life prior to delivery (in which case you may feel baby moving during and after this process).

Your baby's heartbeat will be monitored and you can see this to confirm your baby has died, and you might want to ask for a printout of their heartbeat.

Care for stillbirth

You may notice symptoms of your stillbirth including a discharge, bleeding, your waters breaking early, or a lack of movement from your baby. Or it may be a scan indicating either your baby has died or has a condition that means it is unlikely to survive the pregnancy, birth, or for much time after delivery. You may go into early labour, or arrange a time with the hospital to have your labour induced.

If you are waiting to deliver your baby you may wish to continue with life as usual, or perhaps have some rituals at home to bond with your baby before they are delivered.

I met people who assumed there were no problems and commented on when I was due, which I found really upsetting. I didn't know how best to answer. **Veronica**

If you prefer to continue a pregnancy even though your baby is not going to survive either the full pregnancy or birth (and this is considered a safe option for your health) you may want to continue with the pregnancy as you have been doing. This will mean being monitored, having scans, and connecting with your baby until the time comes to labour naturally, be induced, or have a caesarean section.

I wanted to be with my baby until the end. It was a special and devastating time. **Meena**

I found it difficult to push because I knew when I had the baby they would not be alive and while I knew I had to go through with it I was worried what to expect when they came out. **Valeria**

I knew she wasn't going to live once I had delivered her, but I didn't want to miss any moment of the time she could be with me and I could nourish her. **Coral**

My body was telling me to push, but my brain was saying 'hold on'. **Sue**

You can discuss with your midwives what you want from your birth, what procedures you do or do not want, pain relief options, positions for labour, and what to expect during the delivery and afterwards.

If your baby is likely to survive for a very short time after delivery you may agree with the hospital to take the baby home or to go out for a walk, or somewhere meaningful to you. You should also discuss with your midwife and doctor about resuscitation options so you are prepared for what is feasible, and how that may affect your baby, plus what it would be like to witness. If your baby dies before, during or immediately after birth you may still want time to hold, bathe or dress your baby. Alternatively, due to faith or personal preference you may not want to hold or see your baby and allow the hospital to manage final arrangements.

Seeing your baby

You should be offered the option of seeing your baby. Sometimes you will see your baby during the delivery or immediately after. Some people want to wash their baby, wrap them in a shawl, or dress them. Others prefer healthcare staff to briefly remove the baby and swaddle them with a blanket or clothing you have provided, after which time you can see or hold you baby if you wish. It is entirely your choice. If you are uncertain, tell your midwife or doctor who can give you time in which to make up your mind (in this time your baby will be in a 'cuddle cot' – a refrigerated cot, or hospital mortuary, and they will be brought to you if you want to see them).

66 *We saw our son in his cot, he looked so peaceful.* 99 Michael

66 *Our midwife held our baby and showed her to us.* 99 Afa

66 *Both of us took turns cuddling the twins.* 99 Gill

Some people want to undress and look at their baby, perhaps for reassurance or to see what may have been wrong with them – sometimes it is obvious and sometimes it is not. Your midwife and doctor will explain to you if, before you see your baby, there is anything you need to know. That may include if there are any marks or disfigurations. Again, some people have comfort in seeing their baby no matter how they might appear, but it may also be traumatizing and you have the choice to hold your baby wrapped but covered if you wish this comfort but do not want to look. If there is no possibility of seeing the baby your doctor should let you know why.

You may want to bathe, dress, rock, sing or talk to your baby. Some people want to do this more than once (again you can use a cuddle cot during this time), or to take baby home for a short while to be among friends and family. You may want to take photographs or have someone photograph your baby or you holding your baby. Some people cut a lock of hair to keep.

Chapter 13
(pp. 133–136)

When it is time to say goodbye to your baby you can either let healthcare staff do this (not everyone feels able to manage this parting), and you may want to conduct any final rituals (including faith-based ones if appropriate). You can do this alone, with a partner or with friends and family present.

After loss

After loss you may have many unanswered questions that are difficult to escape from – even if you are given comforting answers from your doctor – more so if you were not. You may wonder if you could have done anything differently or spotted signs sooner, or whether different medical care might have resulted in a happier outcome. And it may be particularly painful if you were aware a loss could happen and you tried to prevent it (for example with surgery, bed rest or other lifestyle changes); or if you felt you had failed because you wanted to keep your baby safe and were unable to. Knowing you were not responsible for your loss may be reassuring – or not bring any relief, as it does not change the realities of your loss.

Physical symptoms

You may still have symptoms – for example you may still look and feel pregnant. Your breasts may feel full and heavy or you may be producing milk (lactating). You will have bleeding for some days or weeks afterwards. You may also experience mood changes, not only due to any trauma you have gone through but also changing hormone levels. Your midwife and doctor should explain these to you, suggest ways to cope, or offer options of reducing milk flow via medication – but if they do not give this information ask them what to expect and what additional care options are open to you.

Emotional reactions

After the delivery of your baby or the funeral or memorial service (if you have one) you may feel a sense of closure – particularly if there has been a period of time spent either not knowing if your pregnancy will end or knowing that it would, or where you were undergoing different tests or making emotionally draining decisions. Some people experience this with a sense of relief, even if they are distressed about losing their baby. Others find it more difficult as they were focused on their loss and now feel bereft, unsettled, or without focus.

Chapter 13
(pp. 137–141)

If there were underlying health problems that led to your loss you may still require treatment for those, and this may add to your feelings of confusion and despair. Talking to your doctor about your prognosis (how your medical condition is liable to progress or manifest itself again in the future) may help you feel more confident about what is happening to you.

You may have had to make choices that were not what you wanted, and made you feel like you had to pick between your own survival and your baby's life. Or that even though you knew the pregnancy was not going to end in a live birth that you still wanted this outcome very much. It is common to feel powerlessness and guilt afterwards, or being proud you were able to manage to navigate healthcare under such harrowing circumstances.

Post mortem

Not all pregnancy losses require a post mortem or other investigations, but you may want to request this – or have it suggested by healthcare staff if you have had several recurrent miscarriages, a late loss, or stillbirth. It is up to you how much detail you are given after a post mortem happens, if you want to ask a lot of questions and read reports that is fine, or you may prefer it to be on your medical records but not for you to consider further.

Following a late loss or stillbirth you may want to see your baby before and after a post mortem. Hospital staff should be sympathetic to your needs and ensure your baby is treated with respect and dignity throughout the process, and when you see them again they are clean and dressed. You will be told what to expect when you see your baby, if for example there are noticeable cuts or stitches. In cases where it is not possible to see your baby again this should be explained to you.

Funeral arrangements

After an early loss, late loss or stillbirth you can arrange a funeral yourself. Hospital staff should look after remains no matter how early the loss happened, but with later losses you may have more involvement in handling your baby (if preferred). A funeral home can help you decide on a burial or cremation and what you might want to happen during the funeral service.

Chapter 13
(pp. 137–141)

Sources
of support
(pp. 145–147)

The hospital can also arrange for burial or cremation – that may be individual (your baby is laid to rest alone) or collectively (several babies are cremated or buried at the same time). Your midwife or doctor should explain what procedures are followed within your hospital to help you decide what you want. You do not have to decide right away and can discuss it with your partner, healthcare staff, pregnancy loss charities, hospital chaplains or your faith leader as needed (see Chapter 13). In some countries or states funerals may be required by law, which may be traumatic if you do not want one. You can raise this with your doctor or faith leader if you do not wish to be involved. The organizations listed in Sources of support might have practical advice and support if you are being pressured into doing things against your wishes.

Going home after loss

Arriving back home may feel reassuring. You are in a safe place you know well and if you have existing children or pets, being back with them may be comforting. Alternatively you may feel unsettled or bewildered about being home without your baby – particularly for a late loss or stillbirth where you have already prepared for baby's arrival. It may be friends, family or your partner remove items that may distress you prior to you coming home – or you may very strongly wish to do this yourself, in your own time.

> ❝ *I couldn't bear to put his cot away for several weeks after. And I still sleep with the blanket he would have used.* ❞ **Kamar**

If you still look or feel pregnant it may be confusing and upsetting, you may be keen to get back to your pre-pregnancy shape as quickly as possible. Or you may resist this as a means of feeling connected with your baby. Both of these reactions, or not being concerned with your appearance at all, are all common.

Being part of your usual routines may also be heartening, but you may also not be able to focus or concentrate or find physical or psychological symptoms continue and disrupt what you were used to before your loss. Accepting recovery can take longer than we expected, that there will be many reminders of your pregnancy and loss (some of which are avoidable and some are not), and to seek help as needed are all good ideas at this time. As is taking things slowly, hour by hour, day by day. There are more ideas in Chapter 8 on how to care for yourself after loss. Chapter 8 (pp. 88–93)

After pregnancy loss see your doctor if you...

- Continue to bleed heavily, or pass clots
- Have pain that is not relieved by painkillers and does not go away
- Have a discharge that is smelly or blood streaked
- Have a temperature of over 100.4°F or 38°C
- Cannot stop crying or have the desire to self-harm or feel suicidal
- Experience distressing flashbacks, intrusive thoughts or nightmares that continue for days, weeks or months
- Have anxiety or depression or if an existing mental health problem is exacerbated by your loss, and that upsets you and interferes with your daily life
- Have persistent feelings of irritability, anger, numbness or hyper alertness that concern you (or others express concern about)
- If you cannot sleep, or if your eating habits change or you cannot concentrate (and this is ongoing, causing you distress, and interfering with your daily life)

How to talk with your partner about your choices

If you are considering your choices for managing miscarriage you may wish to discuss together what options are open to you and how to cope with whichever decision you make. Noting, of course, that ultimately the main decision about managing loss is made by the person who is physically miscarrying. You might want to discuss:

- how you are feeling
- leaflets or information websites explaining more about your pregnancy loss (you may wish to consult these together or read separately)
- your hopes and fears
- seeing the doctor/visiting the hospital together
- using support groups, helplines or charities to clarify any questions or concerns you have
- ideas about how you would like to support each other
- a care plan for the person going through the physical loss (see elsewhere in this chapter)
- the physical and psychological care you are expecting or might need
- what you will do in the future (considering memorializing your loss, see Chapter 13)

Chapter 13
(pp. 133–141)

How to tell friends or family

It is your choice who to tell, in what detail, when, and how. It is a good idea to confide in people you trust and who you know will support you and not breach your confidence nor create a drama or make it all about them. Some people tell lots of friends and relatives, others a select few or none at all. You may want to break the news by phone or email, on social media, or face to face. It is understandable if they are upset – both for you and because they were also looking forward to you having a baby (if they knew of your pregnancy). But if they are really struggling or expecting you to care for them you should point them towards the resources in Sources of support where they can find the support they need.

Sources
of support
(pp. 145–147)

When other people try and help

If people are keen to assist you then you may want to offer them directions so they can give you what you need. That might include:

- giving them a shopping list
- a request for them to help with cleaning or laundry

- asking them to look after any existing children you have
- accepting lifts to hospital or other appointments

It is fine to refuse help if it is not helping you. People talking over you or telling you what to do or what they did is also unhelpful. You have the right to say what you do and do not want.

There is no correct way to act after loss in terms of telling other people. It will not harm your recovery if you choose to say a lot, or a little. But it may be counterproductive if you are made to stay silent or forced to speak up due to other people's thoughtlessness.

> 66 *I called my parents and hers and said 'this may come as a shock but Lin's in hospital having a miscarriage. She is okay physically but I wanted you to know.' I updated them when I knew more.* 99 Jess

> 66 *My sister was so helpful. She asked if I wanted her to break the news and she did so. I don't know what she said but everyone was kind and supportive afterwards.* 99 Ceri

> 66 *We didn't feel able to tell anyone so I wrote my closest friends and family an email explaining Brandon had died, then when we knew they were aware we sent funeral invitations.* 99 Nathan

> 66 *People who were not aware kept asking how the pregnancy was going. They thought 'I'm not pregnant anymore' meant I'd had a live birth. So I said 'I lost the baby'. When they said 'I'm so sorry' I told them I appreciated it. Most did not want to talk but for those who did I was normally okay and when I wasn't I said so.* 99 Matilda

> 66 *Since I'd not told anyone I was pregnant I felt unable to tell them I had lost the baby.* 99 Laila

Talking to existing children (if you have them)

Children that are old enough to understand you have experienced a loss may react in similar ways to you (see Chapter 5). They may be anxious or uncertain, frightened they have done something to cause the loss, or scared they

Chapter 5 (pp. 53–57)

may lose you too. They might be guilty if they had felt jealousy over the pregnancy. Or they may be disappointed or confused if a baby they expected to arrive does not come home. Some children have lots of questions, and younger children particularly may ask these in blunt or insensitive ways. Or they may refuse to discuss it at all. Although you may be upset, they may not be, and should not be blamed if this is the case. If you have more than one child they may react in different ways.

If your child(ren) witnessed your loss they may have been alarmed by it – particularly if there was a lot of blood or you were crying or obviously in pain. Comforting them, reassuring them you are recovering, and being willing to answer any questions they may have is a good idea. They may want to talk to other friends or relatives about what has happened. If they want to know things you do not have the answer to your doctor or the charities listed in Sources of support may be able to help.

Sources of support
(pp. 145–147)

Pregnancy loss can change your regular household routines if there are hospital appointments to get to, or if your children have to stay with friends or relatives while you receive care. Challengingly for you, you may find that tantrums, bed wetting, sleeping or eating issues can reoccur or worsen in younger children; while backchat, nightmares or disruptive behavior may occur in older children and teens.

> 66 *My 3-year-old Khalil was dreadful after my loss. He started wetting and biting. I had hardly any energy to care for myself let alone him. My dad suggested he might be feeling insecure and we focused on making him feel safe. The biting stopped almost right away.* 99 **Darya**

> 66 *I was careful to show Beth that while I was upset, I was not upset with her. Although she is 14 she struggles socially and putting her feelings into words was difficult. I reassured her it was sad but I loved her very much.* 99 **Jo**

Children with existing mental health issues may experience worsening symptoms, while those who are not neurotypical may struggle to process what is happening and you may find it harder than usual to offer them the support you usually give or cope with meltdowns or other behaviours. Children and teenagers with disabilities or special needs may want to know if the baby had similar conditions to theirs, which may bring up additional worries about their own wellbeing and security. Answering in a frank but age-appropriate way is important, while checking your child is not overly anxious (and seeking support if they are).

You can expect some children to be solemn and withdrawn, or wanting to know if they can fix things. They may give age-appropriate responses that seem upsetting to you – talking about when the baby can come home, not understanding the baby has died, or changing the subject or even laughing about very serious issues. Remember this is their way of understanding and/or grieving and trying not to be angry with them or pushing them to feel as you do is important. They are not trying to hurt or disrespect you.

If you are not able to be as focused on your existing children, if you will be in hospital, or you require time to heal physically and psychologically, ensuring other people can support them and you is a good idea. If you have nobody else to assist then social services can arrange temporary care. This happens more than you may think and is not a sign that you are a bad parent, nor that you will have your children removed. It is a reasonable support service to use if you have no other safe or reliable places to go.

It is okay to tell your child you are upset, sad or tired. You do not have to hide your feelings or pretend you are not crying in front of them. Remember, however, not to expect them to manage your grief – if you need support use other services. After stillbirth some older children may want to be involved in saying goodbye. Younger children may struggle to understand, and those with learning difficulties or who are not neurotypical may find the concept of pregnancy loss very difficult to follow. There are resources specifically for children affected by loss at the end of this chapter that may make it easier to explain what is going on.

Chapter 13
(pp. 133–141)

You may want to notify friends, family, teachers or other significant adults in your child(ren)'s lives about how you wish your pregnancy loss to be discussed. That will ensure they do not use phrases or mention issues you are not comfortable with, but do support your child(ren) in ways that are reassuring to you.

Psychological support and where to get it

During pregnancy loss the focus is primarily on your physical treatment, which is what most people specifically need. Having sympathetic and appropriate support from healthcare staff, friends, family, and partners is also important if we are to get over our loss. Help from charities and support groups is also important. Sometimes we also require additional psychological care after pregnancy loss, that may be because:

- there may be fertility problems
- your relationship is adversely affected
- existing mental health problems have worsened
- poor care made the experience of loss more distressing
- you are coping alone, or within a difficult or abusive family situation
- where there is suspected Post Traumatic Stress Disorder (PTSD) or Post Natal Depression (PND)
- there is a history of past abuse that is affecting your ability to cope during and after loss
- you have a disability, learning difficulties, autism or other condition where you need more specific, tailored advice to help you navigate healthcare and other people when dealing with your loss.

Chapter 5 (p. 53) Chapter 5 discusses this in more depth.

Practical issues

Different countries and states have different regulations about maternity and paternity leave and benefit entitlements after loss. For an early (before 12 weeks) and second trimester loss you may not be entitled to maternity or paternity leave, you can request sick leave to recover from any physical procedures and have some time to process what has happened psychologically.

If you have a late loss or stillbirth you may be entitled to maternity and paternity leave, free prescriptions, and statutory maternity benefits (if eligible). You may also be able to apply for hardship grants, maternity grants, and funeral expenses if on a low income, or charities may be able to assist (see Sources of support). Travelling to and from hospital for ongoing testing or monitoring can also introduce hidden costs for transport, childcare (for existing children), parking charges, and time off work. If you are struggling financially due to attending appointments speak to your doctor.

Chapter 5 (pp. 145–147)

Facing the future

Whatever kind of pregnancy loss you experience, the loss itself means all kinds of plans and ideas will change. Whether you wanted to be pregnant or not, and regardless of if your pregnancy was planned or unexpected, being pregnant usually means accepting life is now changing. You are planning to become a parent and will have hopes and dreams for yourself in that role as well as for the baby you are carrying. Coming to terms with your anticipated future no longer existing can be hard to accept and navigate. You may face constant reminders of what might have been, or have to change things you had not expected to do.

66 *I had the room decorated for twins so bringing home one baby was a big adjustment.* 99 **Piper**

66 *I was on maternity leave, but I had to talk to work about returning far earlier. I was expecting to be off for several months but went back six weeks after my stillbirth.* 99 **Zoe**

66 *It's only when you miscarry you realize how many of your hopes, dreams and aspirations are tied up in that tiny bump.* 99 **James**

66 *I've never stopped thinking of myself as a mother, even if people around me don't see me in that way.* 99 **Ewa**

FURTHER HELP

INFORMATION ABOUT PREGNANCY LOSS

A Silent Sorrow. Pregnancy Loss: Guidance and Support for You and Your Family (2nd Ed) (2000). Ingrid Kohn and Perry-Lynn Moffitt with Isabelle A. Wilkins. Routledge.

Miscarriage: What Every Woman Needs to Know (2018). Lesley Regan. Orion Spring.

When A Baby Dies: The Experience of Miscarriage, Stillbirth and Neonatal Death (Revised Ed) (2001). Nancy Kohner and Alix Henley. Routledge.

Not Broken: An Approachable Guide to Miscarriage and Recurrent Pregnancy Loss (2017). Lora Shahine.

The Miscarriage Association has a series of comprehensive and supportive leaflets (in English and other languages) explaining more about early and late miscarriage, ectopic and molar pregnancy and resources on how to cope during and after loss
www.miscarriageassociation.org.uk/information/leaflets

SANDS has information on stillbirth and neonatal death
www.sands.org.uk/support

BEREAVEMENT RESOURCES FOR ADULTS

Cruse Bereavement Care (UK) www.cruse.org.uk

The Miss Foundation https://missfoundation.org

SLOW http://slowgroup.co.uk

The Compassionate Friends www.tcf.org.uk

Grief Journey http://griefjourney.co.uk

TAMBA (Twins and Multiple Births Association) Bereavement Support Group www.tamba.org.uk/bereavement

Grieving Parents Support Network http://grievingparents.net

Grieving Dads https://grievingdads.com

March of Dimes Bereavement Support Kit
www.marchofdimes.org/bereavement-kit-form.aspx and information
on loss and grief
www.marchofdimes.org/complications/loss-and-grief.aspx

Loved Baby: Helping You Grieve and Cherish Your Child after Pregnancy Loss
(2017). Sarah Philpott. BroadStreet Publishing.

RESOURCES FOR CHILDREN AND TEENAGERS

Chapter 12 (Helping Your Children at Home) in *A Silent Sorrow. Pregnancy
Loss: Guidance and Support for You and Your Family* (2nd Ed) (2000). Ingrid
Kohn and Perry-Lynn Moffitt. Routledge has more detailed examples
of what to expect and communication tips for children and teenagers.

I'd Know You Anywhere, My Love (2016). Nancy Tillman. Feiwel and Friends.

Our Baby (Little Ones with Big Questions) (2017). Alma Ravenell. Create
Space.

Wherever You Are My Love Will Find You (2013). Nancy Tillman. Feiwel and
Friends.

Water Bugs and Dragonflies: Explaining Death to Young Children (2004).
Doris Stickney. The Pilgrim Press

Michael Rosen's Sad Book (2011). Michael Rosen and Quentin Blake.
Walker Books.

Childhood Bereavement Network
www.childhoodbereavementnetwork.org.uk

Child Bereavement https://childbereavementuk.org

Winston's Wish www.winstonswish.org

The Pink Elephants Support Network's *Telling the Kids* https://
pinkelephantssupport.com/feel-home/support-resources/telling-children

4. *What to Expect*
FROM HEALTHCARE

This chapter discusses the variety of places you may get help from, and what help healthcare services can offer during and after pregnancy loss. It also addresses what to do if the healthcare you received was inadequate or made the process of coping with miscarriage more difficult and distressing.

Not everyone uses healthcare services for pregnancy loss. That might be because their loss was something they felt able to manage by themselves, or in some countries because there was no affordable doctor available or healthcare was hard to reach. You may or may not have a choice in what doctor cares for you.

Who you may meet – and how they can help
General Practitioner (GP)/family doctor

If you think you are miscarrying your doctor can offer advice in person or over the telephone (if appropriate) and refer you to an Early Pregnancy Unit (EPU) if available, or further specialist care (e.g. a gynaecologist). Your GP or practice nurse can check you are physically recovered following a miscarriage or stillbirth (particularly if you are worried you might have complications post-treatment or an infection). They should also have details of local support groups, local and national pregnancy loss charities, and can also refer you to a counsellor. If you need fertility advice or have concerns about multiple miscarriages they can provide information or refer to other gynaecological or fertility services. Both your GP and practice nurse can give confidential advice if you or your partner has experienced psychosexual problems following pregnancy loss or as a result of fertility worries.

Paramedics

If you experience pregnancy loss at work, while on holiday or at home and need emergency support, you may need the help of paramedics to give immediate care and transport you to hospital. If you are alone and have no way of getting to a hospital by yourself, particularly if you are disabled you should also call for an ambulance.

Accident and Emergency (A&E)/the Emergency Room (ER)

If you experience heavy bleeding and pain, or if your pregnancy loss is happening when you are away from home or outside surgery opening hours, go to Accident and Emergency. On arrival you will be asked by the receptionist what has happened. You or your partner can tell them you are having a miscarriage or stillbirth. It may not always be possible to have a private place to wait but if you need one because you are in a lot of pain, are bleeding heavily or are distressed, then request this. You will see a nurse or doctor who will assess what is going on and you may then be given an internal exam, blood test, and/or an ultrasound (either over your tummy or also inside your vagina). If you are in a lot of pain, are bleeding heavily or feel you are about to pass tissue or your baby, tell the doctor – use the emergency buzzer or call out for help if you are alone and need immediate assistance. You should be given pain relief and you may either be sent home with an appointment to come back for further blood tests and scans; or admitted to the Early Pregnancy Unit, or a gynaecology or women's ward.

If your symptoms worsen between appointments you can call your GP or go back to Accident and Emergency. You should not be seen on a maternity ward, however sometimes due to a lack of facilities or overstretched services this may happen.

Maternity Services/Obstetrics

You may discover you are miscarrying when you have your initial appointment with maternity services, commonly around 12 weeks where a scan may indicate a problem (see Chapter 2); at your 5 month check-up; or at any other point during the pregnancy when you are either having a routine midwife visit or if you make an appointment to see your midwife due to concerns about your pregnancy.

Chapter 2 (p. 10)

Sonographer

Pregnancy loss may be determined by a scan, which is carried out by a sonographer. During a scan you will lie on a coach with the sonographer sitting beside you in front of a computer screen. You will usually keep your clothes on, but you will pull clothing aside so they can put some gel on your stomach (it might feel a little cold) and run the ultrasound over your abdomen (in some countries/hospitals there is a preference for you to wear a gown for this procedure). The sonographer can see on the screen what is inside you. It might be that they notice immediately there is a problem, or it might take them a while. They may also need to scan you internally with a transvaginal ultrasound, a probe that goes inside your vagina – they will use a lubricant for this and it may feel slightly uncomfortable if they are pressing inside you, but tell them if it hurts.

Some sonographers will talk you through what is going on, others will do the scan and then tell you. They may call in a doctor if there is something they are unsure about. If you know you are miscarrying you may have a nurse or doctor in the room with the sonographer; or the midwife or doctor may carry out your scan. You may only need one scan to confirm the pregnancy has ended, or you may need more than one scan and blood test to be certain. If you are preg-nant again in the future (see Chapter 12) you may opt to have a scan prior to 12 weeks at an Early Pregnancy Unit (see below). The experience of discovering

Chapter 12 (pp. 126–127) loss at your scan, particularly if you were excited about your pregnancy and had no indication of your loss, can be very shocking. You may feel numb, disbelieving, or cry or scream. You may be more prepared to expect this if you have had previous losses, but it may not make the news any easier.

Early Pregnancy Unit (EPU)

These services deal with early pregnancy problems, including scans, blood tests and helping those who need it to decide how to manage their miscarriage and ectopic pregnancy. There is more information about what these services offer via the Association of Early Pregnancy Units www.aepu.org.uk (including a map to help you find your nearest unit if you are in the UK). All staff working in Early Pregnancy Units are trained to support you, that may be to reassure you if you are not experiencing a miscarriage, have a history of pregnancy loss, or are miscarrying. Not all hospitals offer this service, and in some countries EPUs do not exist at all. If you feel you need care from an EPU – for example if you are pregnant after previous losses – it is always worth referring yourself, or asking your doctor to do so, as this may not be done routinely.

Bereavement midwife

If you have experienced a late loss or stillbirth you may be offered a Bereavement Midwife. They can assist you during and after your labour, help you decide if you want to spend time with your baby or not, arrange for

Chapter 4 (pp. 25–28) you to have a 'cuddle cot' (also sometimes called a 'cold cot', see Chapter 3) so you can spend more time with your baby; assist with memory boxes, photographs and funerals (see Chapter 13); provide emotional assistance after the funeral (if you decide to have one); and refer you to local support

Chapter 13 (pp. 133–141) charities and groups.

Gynaecologist

You may be referred to gynaecology services if there are complications during or after your miscarriage, ectopic pregnancy or stillbirth. Your GP, EPU or other hospital departments can refer or if you see your gynaecologist privately you can make an appointment yourself.

Counselling/therapy services

Most services you encounter in healthcare do not offer therapy as part of standard care as they are focused more on physical support and treatment. The exception is for late miscarriage and stillbirth where you may have a midwife trained to offer bereavement therapy or where you can be referred to counselling. Your doctor may also be able to refer you to counselling services, although in many countries these are limited and waiting lists may be long. In the UK there are plans to introduce better perinatal mental health services, but how this applies to those who have experienced pregnancy loss remains to be seen. You can also refer yourself, but will have to pay – remember, however, many therapists offer a sliding scale of fees. Most people use counselling services after their loss to help them cope with trauma, grief, and despair (see Chapter 5). You can use counselling services immediately after loss, or any time afterwards (even decades later). Some therapists recommend you do not have counseling during or right after loss, allowing yourself time to experience any emotional reactions that are entirely appropriate. It might be you prefer individual therapy, go with your partner, or join a therapy group.

Chapter 5 (pp. 53–57)

Navigating care

When you see a doctor, nurse, midwife or other health professional they will want to take a history from you to find out what is going on. You may find you have to answer the same things with different health workers so having a list of answers to share with them can be useful. Even if questions seem repetitive and intrusive remember they are being asked to ensure you get the most appropriate care, and staff should be sensitive to this.

You can expect to be asked things like:

How old are you?
What was the date of your last menstrual period? (it does not have to be precise if you cannot exactly remember)
How did you get pregnant? (e.g. natural or assisted conception)
How many weeks is your current pregnancy? (they may say 'how far along are you?')

Have you been pregnant before?

Have you had a miscarriage, ectopic pregnancy or stillbirth previously? When did they happen?

Do you have any children? What are their ages? How is their physical health?

If you have given birth before, did you have any pregnancy or delivery complications? How did you deliver your baby/babies?

What contraception have you used in the past? Do you want to discuss contraception today?

Who is your doctor? Have you had any previous care for this pregnancy/loss?

Do you have any existing health problems?

Do you have any mental health issues?

Are you taking any medication currently? If so, what?

Do you drink alcohol? How much per week?

Do you smoke? How many cigarettes per day? (let them know if you vape)

Do you use any prescription or recreational drugs? Which ones and how often?

Are you in a relationship?

Is your relationship okay, any problems there?

What support do you have from your partner, friends or family?

Is there anything you would like to ask me, or need me to know?

They should also ask you if you prefer to see them alone (without a partner, friends or family present). You can indicate this if you want to, if you need privacy or your relationship is abusive, or family are controlling. Or if you want support you can ask to have someone with you.

> 66 *I made a list of symptoms and questions and took it to all my appointments.* 99 Phoebe

During pregnancy loss it is easy to feel out of control, afraid, frustrated, and uncertain. It is okay to be assertive about your needs and preferences when receiving healthcare.

WHAT YOU CAN REQUEST FROM HEALTHCARE

- to see a doctor or nurse who is the same gender as you
- a private room to talk to healthcare staff
- accessible facilities if you are disabled
- time to process what has happened and reflect on your options
- clear information about what has happened – and will happen – in terms of your physical and emotional reactions and clinical care. This may be requested verbally or in writing, including easy-read versions if you require it, or specific information tailored to your needs if you are autistic or neurodiverse
- not to have medical students present (or to include them in your care if you prefer)
- to have your partner, friends or family members present
- interpreters – someone who can help if you are speaking a different language to healthcare staff (including sign language)
- advocates (if you have a learning difficulty) and chaperones (if you are alone and want support)
- a second opinion, or to see another practitioner to help explain if you are unclear what you are being told; or to discuss options if you change your mind about your care
- further tests and scans
- care and understanding if you have experienced previous losses or problems with care in the past
- support from chaplaincy services
- the opportunity to ask questions (and to do so more than once)
- recommendations for print or online materials that explain what is going on, or referrals to local charities and support groups (see also Sources of support)
- written information about what the doctor has told you
- a clear understanding of what is going to happen from start to finish.

Chapter
(pp. 145–147)

Honouring these requests may not always be possible depending on when and where you are accessing services and if you require emergency care, but you are not a passive person in all this; it is your right to have care that is clearly explained, respects your choices, and maintains your dignity.

Things you can ask healthcare staff about

Here are some of the questions people have told me they have raised with healthcare staff during or after their pregnancy loss, that you may want to ask about too.

Why has this happened?
Did I do anything to cause it?
Will it happen again?
When can I try and get pregnant again?
I can't stop crying and I don't think I'll ever feel better, can you help me?
The loss was really traumatic, is it normal to keep remembering the details?
I've had several miscarriages, should I see a specialist now?
Are there any symptoms I should be aware of after my loss?
Can you recommend any other charities or support groups to help me cope?
Is there anything I should or shouldn't do to help my recovery?
When can I bathe again?
I am in a lot of physical or psychological pain – what should I do?
Is there anything I should change about my lifestyle to help me get pregnant in the future?

Being in hospital

If you seek medical care from your family doctor or hospital you are inevitably going to be in the company of other patients and visitors. Ordinarily this may not be an issue for you, but during or after loss it might be significant and upsetting as it might include:

- seeing or hearing other people who are losing a pregnancy
- being on a ward or in a clinic with people who have other gynaecological conditions (e.g. having a hysterectomy)
- being among other people who are having happier news about their pregnancies and who may assume you are in the same situation (if your miscarriage is disclosed while you are using Maternity Services)
- seeing or hearing people in labour, hearing newborn babies crying, or seeing families and newborns (maternity clinics and even Early Pregnancy Units can be located near maternity wards and delivery suites)

Usually healthcare staff are sensitive about this and can help you avoid interacting with people whose pregnancy news is different from yours, or offer greater support to you if this is not possible.

If you miscarry after being registered with a hospital you may well still get follow-up calls from midwives or letters from the hospital, assuming you are still pregnant. Anticipating this may happen will not necessarily stop it being upsetting or unnerving, but it reduces it coming as a shock.

THINGS YOU MAY WANT TO TAKE WITH YOU IF YOU ARE GOING TO HOSPITAL

- A change of clothes
- Several pairs of knickers
- Nightwear and dressing gown, or tracksuit/T-shirt and jogging bottoms
- Extra absorbent sanitary towels
- Toothbrush, toothpaste and deodorant
- Beauty products and makeup
- Shower gel
- Flip flops (for communal showers)
- Your own phone, or change to use the public phone
- Books, magazines or other things to keep you occupied
- Money to pay for hospital television
- Snacks

How partners may experience healthcare

As Chapter 7 explains, partners often act as advocates and assistants during healthcare encounters. They may be the ones discussing symptoms, explaining details about the pregnancy or your medical history – particularly if you are unable to; or trying to keep track of what is going on while conveying this information to other relatives or friends. Ideally anyone experiencing miscarriage should be treated with compassion and care, but partners report they are often sidelined, neglected, or made to feel their needs and concerns are secondary. If you are a partner it is okay to ask the same questions about care as covered above (or other concerns you might have) and you should also feel able to express yourself without having to hide your emotions. If you are asked to do things by healthcare staff you do not feel able to offer, it is important to say you cannot help and ask for other support. You may find the trauma of witnessing miscarriage or stillbirth is very difficult to cope with and asking for additional care, explanations about what is going on or reassurance about your loved one's wellbeing are all appropriate things to do (see Chapter 7).

Chapter 7
(pp. 75–77)

Chapter 7
(pp. 78–83)

Standards of care during pregnancy loss

Not everyone experiences healthcare positively. It may be previous experiences of healthcare for other conditions, or past pregnancy losses have been poor; leaving you feeling mistrustful or anxious about current care. Or the physical or psychological support offered during or after your miscarriage was not delivered properly.

Young parents may have felt judged and shamed during their pregnancy or in care during and after their loss – perhaps being told their losses were 'for the best'. While Black, Indigenous or other People of Colour may have been discriminated against by healthcare providers or struggle to access basic care, leaving them feeling unconfident when seeking help. Racial stereotyping can also mean referrals to support services are not made, adequate pain relief is not provided, or incorrect assumptions are made by healthcare staff – for example that minorities are fertile so will have no problems conceiving again, or that minorities are resilient, requiring no additional assistance.

Those who are disabled, have a chronic illness, are not neurotypical, or have mental health problems may face intrusive questions; a lack of clear information about their specific needs; remarks about pregnancy loss being a good thing; or a lack of clarity about trying again (particularly if assisted conception is needed).

Lesbian, Bi or Trans people may experience excluding care where the unique needs of same-sex parents or diverse relationships are stigmatized or judged. Where there have been multiple losses or you have used fertility treatments the investment of time, money, and energy in getting pregnant may be especially difficult to cope with and healthcare staff may not always appreciate the magnitude of this – suggestions of 'you can always try again' may be unrealistic.

Ideally healthcare should be compassionate, clearly explained, and non-stigmatizing – but in cases where it is delivered poorly or thoughtlessly this may add to or worsen the initial distress of miscarriage. Indeed, for some people (including me) the miscarriage was something they could cope with – but poor care was not.

There are a number of different guides about care standards during and after miscarriage, ectopic pregnancy, and stillbirth. These can vary across organisations, health trusts, charities, and within and between different countries. Most of these recommendations agree principles including:

"The nurse thought I was her sister"

- offering *clinically correct, clearly explained, respectful and compassionate care* delivered in a *timely fashion*
- with *appropriate referrals* and *early diagnosis*
- given in a way that *best suits the needs and circumstances of the individual.*

Several codes are listed at the end of this chapter, while the charities listed in Sources of support have links to specific guidance or recommendations for good care you may wish to consult, or you can ask your hospital if they have their own guidance.

Sources of support (pp. 145–147)

The care you get should make your loss as easy to manage as possible, not worsen it. Noting that negative reactions to healthcare may have little to do with the quality of care you have been given and more to do with your wider feelings about your loss is important. Sometimes infections or complications are unavoidable and you should have all risks and benefits of treatment options explained to you.

Self-help books often present best-case scenarios, ignoring how poor care may exist and the damage it does. I would love to say all care during and after pregnancy loss is appropriately and compassionately delivered. But it is not. Across the world there remains a need to improve clinical and psychological care for pregnancy loss. So you should complain to the hospital if information was not conveyed to you appropriately, if staff were judgemental or unsupportive, or if you were pushed to do things you did not want to. You can do this via letter, going via the hospital complaints procedure, speaking to organisations like Patient Advice and Liaison Service (PALS) (if available), or direct to professional councils (for nurses, doctors, sonographers). This can obviously be exhausting and upsetting, and sometimes may be an outlet for other feelings around loss but not necessarily accurate (for example, you

Sources
of support
(pp. 145–147)

want to sue the hospital because you are angry that you lost your baby but not because they offered substandard care). Talking about your feelings and experiences with the charities and support groups listed in Sources of support can help you cope effectively, move on if there is no cause for further action, or bring a complaint in the right way via the appropriate channels.

FURTHER HELP

GENERAL HEALTH INFORMATION

NHS Choices www.nhs.uk

Patient https://patient.info

Our Bodies Ourselves www.ourbodiesourselves.org

Health Direct www.healthdirect.gov.au

Healthlink www.healthlinkbc.ca

Centres for Disease Control and Prevention (CDC) www.cdc.gov

CARE GUIDELINES

Pregnancy Loss and the Death of a Baby: Guidelines for Professionals (4th Ed). (2016). SANDS (Stillbirth and Neonatal Death Charity) [While aimed at professionals this is a comprehensive guide and may be worth reading if you require medical information about your loss].

SANDS *principles of bereavement care*
www.uk-sands.org/professionals/principles-bereavement-care/sands-principles-bereavement-care

Royal College of Obstetricians and Gynaecologists (RCOG) UK *Checklist for Respectful Care in Women's Health* (2017)
www.rcog.org.uk/globalassets/documents/global-network/policy-and-advocacy/respectful-care/respectful-care-checklist.pdf

MMBRACE-UK (Mothers and Babies: Reducing Risk through Audits and Confidential Enquiries Across the UK)
www.npeu.ox.ac.uk/mbrrace-uk

National Bereavement Care Pathway (NBCP) UK
www.nbcpathway.org.uk

Death Before Birth Project https://deathbeforebirthproject.org

National Institute for Health and Clinical Excellence (NICE) *guidance on ectopic miscarriage and miscarriage*
www.nice.org.uk/guidance/cg154

NICE *Guidance on Suspected and Confirmed Miscarriage*
https://cks.nice.org.uk/miscarriage

NICE Guidance on Antenatal and Postnatal Health
www.nice.org.uk/guidance/cg192

Cross Country *Guidance on Managing Miscarriage*
www.gfmer.ch/Guidelines/Infertility_miscarriage_ectopic_
pregnancy/Infertility_miscarriage_ectopic_pregnancy_mt.htm

World Health Organization *Guidance on Preconception, Pregnancy, Childbirth and Postpartum Care*
https://extranet.who.int/rhl/topics/preconception-pregnancy-childbirth-and-postpartum-care/miscarriage

Appendix 2 – *Principles of Good Practice* in *When A Baby Dies: The Experience of Late Miscarriage, Stillbirth and Neonatal Death* (Revised Ed) (2001). Nancy Kohner and Alix Henley. Routledge.

Sources
of support
(pp. 145–147)

ORGANIZATIONS WORKING TOWARDS IMPROVED CARE DURING AND AFTER PREGNANCY LOSS

Aside from those listed in Sources of support, the following organizations may be worth consulting if you want more information on quality care (or to recommend your doctor, midwife or hospital utilizes):

Tommy's www.tommys.org/our-organisation/help-and-support

Pregnancy Loss and Infant Death Alliance (PLIDA) http://plida.org

Resolve Through Sharing
www.gundersenhealth.org/resolve-through-sharing

Shoshana Center www.shoshanacenter.com

5. *Your Emotions*
DURING AND AFTER PREGNANCY LOSS

This chapter deals with how you may feel, and how to cope mentally during and after pregnancy loss.

Common responses to pregnancy loss

GRIEF AND DISTRESS

This may be overwhelming and manifest itself in crying and sobbing, feeling sick, having a sense of dread or feeling of emptiness inside, a pain in your chest, feeling shivery and cold, or your body may physically ache. (It is important to note sometimes these feelings may be the symptoms of an infection, so if you have physical reactions alongside those listed in Chapter 2 you should see your doctor.)

SOLUTIONS

Accept this is an understandable reaction to pain and trauma and best approached as you would any bereavement and shock (see Chapter 8 for more ideas).

EMOTIONAL UPHEAVAL

You may struggle to fall asleep, have unsettled nights or wake early. You may completely lose your appetite or comfort eat. You may be easily distracted and struggle to concentrate.

SOLUTIONS

Try and rest even if you are not able to sleep. Identify calming things you can do if awake. Allow friends or family to help with cooking. Soups, smoothies or shakes may be palatable and easy to digest if you do not wish to eat much. Or eat whatever you fancy if you are struggling with your appetite. If you have an eating disorder and your loss has triggered it seek help from your GP or www.beateatingdisorders.org.uk

Chapter 2 (p. 8)

Chapter 8 (pp. 88–93)

UNCERTAINTY

You may not understand why you miscarried or have unanswered questions about your loss that leaves you feeling frustrated and bewildered. You may also not know if or when you want to try again (see Chapter 11).

Chapter 11 (pp. 110–112)

SOLUTIONS

Accept these concerns are a predictable part of recovery after loss, but if you wish to know more about what is happening to you then speak to your doctor or use the support groups listed in Sources of support.

Sources of support (pp. 145–147)

FEAR

You may be frightened you will not get pregnant in the future, that you will experience pregnancy loss again, or have alarming intrusive thoughts and memories about what happened during your loss.

SOLUTIONS

Chapter 8 (pp. 88–93)

Try self-care and calming strategies (see Chapter 8). Seek support from healthcare staff, and the charities and organisations listed in Sources of support.

Sources of support (pp. 145–147)

Appreciate that fear is normal – if you are anxious about what has happened to your baby or to you, and what is liable to happen in the future it is understandable you will be stressed.

ANGER

This may be directed at your body for not doing as you want it to, towards other people who are pregnant or have children, or to your partner, friends and family if you feel unsupported. It may present itself as feelings of envy and jealousy, or rage.

SOLUTIONS

Venting in ways that help you may release some of these feelings. Other people have tried sport and exercise as a means of letting off steam; writing diaries, letters, stories or poems about how you feel; listening to music; yelling and shouting; crying; punching a pillow.

Noting your anger is a reasonable response. Why shouldn't you feel angry about losing something you wanted?

PANIC

Feelings of anxiety and stress may leave you highly agitated about what has happened, what you need to do, and even everyday activities suddenly feel overwhelming and difficult.

SOLUTIONS

Talk to your doctor if you are overwhelmed by feelings of anxiety, or if you are having panic attacks contact www.anxietyuk.org.uk

DESPAIR

You may feel as if everything is going wrong, that part of your life is missing, or that there is no hope or chance for things to be happy in the future.

SOLUTIONS

All of these reactions are understandable. They usually feel less acute over time but if you are concerned about suicidal feelings or you cannot move past these emotions you may want to use the services listed under *In an Emergency* in Chapter 2.

FAILURE

If others were aware of the pregnancy, and your partner, family and friends were excited and looking forward to having a baby, you may feel like the loss has somehow let them down, or that you are a disappointment.

SOLUTIONS

Recognizing others can feel sad or disappointed without it reflecting on you is valuable.

DENIAL

It may be difficult for you to comprehend your pregnancy has ended, particularly if you still have symptoms. You might even struggle to believe you are not going to have a baby; or refuse to talk about any aspect of your loss, perhaps acting instead as if you never were pregnant at all.

SOLUTIONS

This may be an important way to cope and could get you through the early weeks and months after loss. However, if you, your partner or other friends or family member notices you are deteriorating, or seem deluded or confused, you should see your doctor or go to the ER/A&E.

Chapter 2
(pp. 12–13)

RELIEF

If you did not want to be pregnant, had concerns about being pregnant within a relationship that was in crisis, were unsure you could cope with parenthood, or were planning to terminate your pregnancy, then a miscarriage may be welcomed, or at least not be a cause for upset.

SOLUTIONS

If your miscarriage was a relief then you may not need additional help, but if you want support because you are worried you are wrong for feeling as you do or just want to talk over aspects of your loss, the charities listed in Sources of support will listen without judgement.

Sources of
support
(pp. 145–147)

NUMBNESS

During and after pregnancy loss you may feel completely numb and shut off from your feelings, even if you are experiencing physical pain. It may be difficult to talk or open up to other people, or to cry or show other emotions.

SOLUTIONS

This will usually pass within a matter of days, weeks or months after loss. If you are not noticing any change and this troubles you then speak to your doctor.

Sources of
support
(pp. 145–147)

BEING MATTER OF FACT

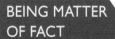

Some people accept they have had a loss, and while they are sad about it, they do not feel overly bothered by it. This may be because they know miscarriage is common and believe they will be pregnant in the future, or where they have coped with pregnancy loss before.

SOLUTIONS

If this approach helps you then continue as you are. However, if you are acting this way to cover up your distress, or feel you have no choice if nobody around you is sympathetic (or there is no support network) then the support groups listed in Sources of support may be worth consulting.

RESENTMENT

Wherever you go there may be reminders of pregnancy – seeing bumps everywhere, people with new babies; or pregnancy, birth and parenthood being the topic of conversation among friends or family or in TV dramas, books and movies. You may also feel resentful of those you know have had a loss but are supported by their partner, family, and friends if you have not received this care, or feel aggrieved if you did not receive adequate healthcare.

SOLUTIONS

This may be an undesirable reaction, but is common and understandable. You may decide to vent elsewhere (see above), or to use support groups (see Sources of support).

HOPE

You may feel certain that in the future, whether you have a baby or not, things will work out for you.

SOLUTIONS

This may be a feeling you want to share with others, or keep to yourself. You may wish to record your thoughts in a diary or notes, or find other ways to stay inspired and motivated.

Just as pregnancy loss can be experienced in different ways by different people, if you have had more than one loss you may find you react differently for each one. Some might be easier to deal with than others, you may have a better idea of what to expect and so can navigate healthcare, or it may be with every loss you become more distressed. There is no correct way to respond to multiple losses and you should not feel guilty if you find with each pregnancy you are less enthusiastic than before, or if you become matter of fact and detached about your losses.

Reactions that may seem overwhelming

Some people can also experience flashbacks or symptoms of PTSD after miscarriage (or in future pregnancies or even birth following pregnancy after loss). These may not be particularly logical but can be very intense. You may vividly recall the sights, sounds, smells or the feeling of your loss. It might be like replaying what has happened, or more disconnected sensations that are distressing but hard to explain or place.

❝ The sound of ambulance sirens takes me back every time I hear them. ❞ Sharon

❝ I can't handle the sight or smell of blood anymore. ❞ Tim

❝ My loss started at work. The first time I went back there it felt very weird. ❞ Haloke

❝ I know I can't avoid seeing women's bumps, but it seems like they're everywhere at the moment. ❞ Maryam

Worries about reaching out

You may be concerned about asking for help even if you are struggling to cope; particularly if you have symptoms of anxiety, depression or other severe mental illness or PTSD. Or you may believe you should be able to manage or will be okay in time – although it is clear that you are deteriorating. Stigma about mental health also means we are unwilling to admit to mental distress for fear of being labelled 'mad', being hospitalized, or otherwise shunned or excluded. Many parents I've spoken to revealed they put off seeking help for fear their existing children might be removed or if they were to get pregnant again their baby would be taken from them after birth.

Alternatively, financial difficulties and fears over losing your job or benefits may be a barrier. You can get information about managing your money and employment rights from:

Citizens Advice www.citizensadvice.org.uk
National Debtline www.nationaldebtline.org
Money Advice Service www.moneyadviceservice.org.uk/en
Turn 2 Us www.turn2us.org.uk
Quaker Social Action www.quakersocialaction.org.uk
Social Security Rights Victoria www.ssrv.org.au

All of these worries are understandable, but it is worth noting the sooner you get help the quicker support can be offered. Advice is confidential and if you need additional mental health care this will be seen in context of your loss and not be taken as any indicator of your ability to be a good parent now, or in the future.

*" I was scared to tell my GP
I was depressed, but she said
my reactions were to be expected
and was glad I told her.
I wish I had done so sooner. "*

Blake

*" I had previously been
sectioned and was anxious this
might happen again. I explained
to my doctor how sad I felt and
was given more support. I didn't
have to go back to hospital but I
felt less anxious about it. "* **Liv**

FURTHER HELP

The book *Coping With Infertility, Miscarriage and Neonatal Loss: Finding Perspectives and Creating Meaning.* Amy Wenzel (2014) American Psychological Association is a very comprehensive and reassuring guide to understanding your feelings, and coping with your emotions – including ones that may feel self-destructive or disturbing. The text includes a number of worksheets to complete that may help you feel more resilient.

GENERAL MENTAL HEALTH

Mental Health SOS Guide (Rethink)
www.rethink.org/about-us/mental-health-sos

MIND www.mind.org.uk

SANE www.sane.org.uk

Mental Health Foundation www.mentalhealth.org.uk

Anxiety UK www.anxietyuk.org.uk

PANDAS (pre and postnatal depression advice and support)
www.pandasfoundation.org.uk

CALM (Campaign Against Living Miserably)
www.thecalmzone.net

International Mental Health First Aid Programs
www.mhfainternational.org/international-mhfa-programs.html

Get Self Help www.getselfhelp.co.uk

South African Depression and Anxiety Group www.sadag.org

Aboriginal and Torres Strait Islander Mental Health and Maori Mental Health resources
www.ranzcp.org/Publications/Indigenous-mental-health.aspx

YOU MIGHT ALSO WANT TO TRY THESE APPS:

Living Life to the Full www.llttf.com

Headspace www.headspace.com

MoodTools www.moodtools.org

BIRTH TRAUMA

Solace for Mothers www.solaceformothers.org

Birth Trauma Association www.birthtraumaassociation.org.uk

TRAUMA RECOVERY AND PTSD SUPPORT

PTSD UK www.ptsduk.org

Assist Trauma Care http://assisttraumacare.org.uk

After Trauma www.aftertrauma.org

Trauma Survivors Network www.traumasurvivorsnetwork.org

PTSD Association of Canada www.ptsdassociation.com

Phoenix Australia http://phoenixaustralia.org

6. *Making Sense of*
WHAT HAS HAPPENED

Why me?

It can be really difficult to process why you have lost a baby. You may be wondering why this has happened to you, particularly if it has occurred more than once. Or why other people have stayed pregnant and delivered a live baby when you have not.

Did I make this happen?

In trying to make sense of pregnancy loss, you may search around for possible causes. Often this can lead you back to blaming yourself. When I've run workshops with we've discovered all of us thought we might have caused our losses by doing things like:

> *Drinking alcohol.*
> *Exercising, dancing or other physical activity.*
> *Having arguments because of relationship*
>   *problems.*
> *Work or overwork.*
> *Going on holiday or travelling.*
> *Putting off having a baby.*
> *Not dealing with stress or other problems.*

More taboo topics that people do not want to talk about so openly include using recreational drugs; having sex, using sex toys, masturbating and/or experiencing orgasm; cheating; having negative thoughts about their pregnancy; or being in contact with someone who has also lost a baby.

"Could it be because of exercise?"

"We had sex!"

Could I have stopped it?

This is an understandable reaction, and it may be reassuring to note that once a loss has started there is usually little or nothing that can prevent it. Accepting you neither caused nor could have prevented your loss may be a vital message to keep repeating to yourself – and to others if you are in the unfortunate position of being accused or blamed by them. However, you may find yourself doubting what happened and whether things could have been different, which may persist even if logically you know not to fault yourself.

"Was it because I smoked?"

"I didn't know I was pregnant so was drinking a lot"

If only I hadn't...

Similar to questioning whether you might have been able to prevent your loss, you may fret about the things you did prior. Even if you accept you did not cause the loss you may still wish things had happened differently

> 66 *I wish I had not told so many people I was pregnant because telling them I wasn't anymore was really horrible.* 99 Stephanie

> 66 *We were given so many gifts for the baby, which I know was kind, but not having them there when I came home from hospital would have been much easier.* 99 Nicole

Am I being punished?

Some people fear miscarriage is a sign of punishment, revenge, ill-wishing or retribution. Other fears include that you have done something to your baby and therefore can't talk about the miscarriage in case of being blamed.

Sometimes partners may be concerned that they have brought about the miscarriage by not being enthusiastic enough about the pregnancy, or because of ways they have acted in the past (including cheating or relationship breakups)

> 66 *I told her I wasn't sure about the pregnancy, and then she lost our baby. I should've kept my mouth shut.* 99 Callum

What can cause pregnancy loss?

You may be very keen to know what might have caused your loss – either to make sense of it now; to prevent it happening again in the future; or to consider if you need additional testing, treatment or support.

Chromosomal abnormalities

When sperm and egg meet and cells divide there is always a chance for extra or missing chromosomes, which means the pregnancy ends or does not develop normally. Most often chromosomal abnormalities happen by chance, and will not repeat in future. But if you are older, or have previously miscarried due to suspected or known chromosomal abnormality your doctor may recommend prenatal testing or an amniocentesis (where cells are sampled from the amniotic fluid during the 15–20 week of pregnancy via needle directed by an ultrasound image).

Pre-existing or undiagnosed health conditions

In most cases, if you already have a recognized physical or mental health problem for which you are receiving care and medication you may be asked about your plans for future pregnancies, or will seek medical advice prior to trying to conceive. Conditions such as epilepsy, lupus, high blood pressure, sickle cell disease, kidney disease and diabetes can cause complications during pregnancy and during birth. If you experienced miscarriage or stillbirth and have these conditions you may want to discuss with your doctor and midwife ways to reduce risks to future pregnancies (if desired) while maintaining your wellbeing.

Problems with your uterus or cervix

You may have been born with reproductive organs that differ from the norm. These can be detected through physical examinations, ultrasound or laproscopic investigation. For example you may have more than one cervix or uterus, or what's unflatteringly called an '*incompetent cervix*', meaning there's a weakness in the cervix that leads it to open too soon – causing early birth. Or you may develop problems with your uterus or cervix – a commonly observed condition here is fibroids (usually benign tumours that grow inside your womb) that can be removed surgically. Cervical weakness can be treated with a 'cervical stitch' (cerclage), where the cervix is sutured between weeks 14 to 16 weeks of pregnancy and those stitches removed towards the end of pregnancy in week 36 onwards.

There may also be problems with the placenta, including not giving enough nutrients to the baby (placental insufficiency); lack of blood flow from placenta to baby (placental infarction); where the placenta comes away from the uterus before birth (placental abruption); or a low-lying placenta (placenta praevia). If these occur then you may be offered the option of an autopsy/post mortem and investigations of placenta and baby; closer monitoring for future pregnancies; or counseling if it is likely the problem might reoccur.

"I got pregnant by accident"

"I didn't want to be pregnant"

Hormonal problems

During pregnancy, as you may have already noticed, a number of hormones are produced and problems may occur if the body does not make enough hormones to help you get and stay pregnant. If you have polycystic ovaries, or other hormonal problems, this may increase your risk of miscarriage and affect your fertility.

Diabetes or thyroid conditions that are controlled through medication and diet should not prevent you from getting or staying pregnant (although again you will want careful monitoring and support from healthcare staff and midwives during pregnancy, birth and the antenatal period). Poorly controlled diabetes, or other health conditions that are not medicated nor supported can contribute to pregnancy loss and if this was the case for you there may be relief the pregnancy is over, or distress and guilt over your loss.

Acquired illnesses, infections, and accidents

All of us worry about getting sick in pregnancy, although reassuringly most of us recover, with no ill-effect to baby. There are, however, a number of viral infections that can cause early miscarriage, affect the developing fetus, or can be passed on to a newborn, including *HIV, Genital Herpes, Zika*, and *German Measles* (also known as Rubella – which in most western countries people are routinely innoculated against). You may be offered routine testing for these infections, but if you are not sure tell your midwife so appropriate arrangements can be made for testing, treatment and support during your pregnancy, birth, and care of your new baby. Bacterial infections include *Brucella* (the reason you're advised to avoid contact with sheep and goats that may carry this infection); *listeria* (why unwashed fruit and vegetables, meat pates and unpasturized cheese are off the menu in pregnancy); and *salmonella* (why pregnant women are encouraged to avoid raw eggs and unpasturized cheese). Plus parasitic infections such as *malaria* (affecting many women in low-income countries, and why travellers are recommended to avoid malaria areas while pregnant or to take anti-malarials strictly as prescribed), and *toxoplasmosis* (why you're advised not to clean out the cat litter tray while pregnant).

Sadly some accidents cause pregnancy loss – most commonly road traffic accidents, falls, or physical assault. Again, pregnancies can often survive injuries that happen outside the womb, but in cases where accident contributed to your loss you may be traumatized both by the accident, your injuries, and your loss. The suggestions for support recommended in Chapter 5 (including PTSD

Chapter 5 (pp. 57–61)

resources) may be useful, as may assistance from the police, legal advice, and in the case of abuse domestic violence agencies (see later in this chapter).

Problems during labour and delivery

Stillbirth may occur if the baby has already died, but this could also occur during labour and birth. This might include problems with the placenta (see above); prolapsed umbilical cord (where the cord is passed before the baby and trapped by the baby during passage down the vagina during delivery), or where the cord wraps around baby's neck; or birth asphyxia (where baby does not breathe). Losing a baby that was otherwise healthy during pregnancy can be devastating and hospital staff should do all they can to support you in such a case. If your baby dies during labour you will be offered the option of an autopsy/post mortem and there should be an investigation about what occurred during labour in terms of healthcare provided and any interventions offered or given to identify the cause of death. You may also need legal advice. Sadly deaths due to negligence and malpractice do occur and you may find specific assistance from the stillbirth and trauma charities listed in Sources of support worth considering.

Sources
of support
(pp. 145–147)

When healthcare staff say 'I don't know'

This drove me to distraction after my losses. I wanted to know more about what had happened, and why. But was given the same reply, *'we don't know'* or *'it's just one of those things'*. If you want to know what is going on and are not getting answers you can follow it is okay to ask for clarification. *'Don't know'* could translate as there might be many possible reasons for your loss (in which case ask what these might be and which is most likely to apply to you); or doctors cannot tell what has happened without further tests (in which case check if these are necessary and if so what they involve); or they are just not sure what has happened to you (there isn't always a clear reason).

Calming your inner critic and silencing those endless questions

There are many ways to try and cope with the way you feel during and after pregnancy loss. Suggestions recommended by others who have been in the same situation as you include:

Accepting you may always wonder – over time you may have less of an acute reaction to your loss and fewer questions running around in your head. But you may always have concerns there was either something you did to cause your loss, or something that may have prevented it.

Discover more about pregnancy loss – that might be in reading this book or the resources recommended throughout and in Sources of support. You may be reassured by finding out as much as possible about loss to remind yourself you were not to blame. Sources of support (pp. 145–147)

Deciding not to learn more – not everyone is comforted by information and facts. It can feel more confusing or triggering to read other people's accounts of loss or different resources or fact sheets that still do not give you the specific answers to your questions about loss.

Blocking negative thoughts – following a stressful situation it is understandable you will be shocked and uncertain. Having statements to say to yourself, or even written down or stored on your phone where you can find or see them can break the ongoing mental cycle of blame.

> *When I start up with the self-blame I say STOP! or NOT NOW! really loudly in my head (and sometimes even out loud). It lets me notice what I am doing.* Becky

> *I remind myself I'd never say this to a friend that had miscarried, so why do I say it to myself?* Kuvam

> *I have written a card to myself full of the kind things I would say to someone else that had miscarried, including how I am not to blame and that I am a good person. When I have a wobble I get it out and read it.* Trinity

"I thought I miscarried because I was too old"

"I thought I was too young"

Dealing with other people

Just as everyone seems to have an opinion about what you ought to be doing while you are pregnant, so people have their own ideas about your loss. This can be reassuring if they are able to tell you not to be hard on yourself, or remind you they have felt exactly as you do. Friends or family who can listen and not judge while you share your feelings about your loss – no matter how bizarre they may be – can be really useful during and after pregnancy loss.

However, there can be times when explanations are not helpful nor welcome. You can expect people, often with the best intentions, to tell you things about not blaming yourself, trying again or make claims about how you will be okay for future pregnancies. This may not be much comfort, or can even be more distressing if you have had multiple losses or suspect you have fertility problems. When you are angry or grieving even the kindest comments can feel like an attack.

If you don't want to talk about your loss you can state you do not want to discuss it further. For example, *'We are sorry to tell you that we recently lost our baby. We appreciate your love at this time but we really are not up to discussing it.'* It might be easier to do this in a card or email or over the phone. If, during conversations people make inappropriate, intrusive or tactless comments – or just raise things you do not want to discuss – you can respond with:

Thank you, I am sure that worked for you but it isn't really helping me.
I don't feel able to discuss this now.
It is too painful for me to talk about this.
Let's change the subject.
That wasn't the case for me.

Or even a very straightforward *'no'*. It isn't rude to ask for people to discuss things in ways that do not distress you; to correct them if they are wrong; and if people continue to press when you have asked them not to then being more assertive, ending the conversation or leaving/asking them to leave is absolutely fine.

If you are in work, your employer should be sympathetic about your circumstances, offering time off for you to recover physically and emotionally, and attend to funerals or other medical appointments. Your doctor can also help you navigate this process. Not everyone wants to tell their employer about pregnancy loss, particularly if you're new to a job or on a precarious contract. However, most people do find if they ask for help or time off it is sympathetically given and colleagues are generally supportive. You may find it easier to notify one person who tells others in your workplace, or ask a partner or family member to alert work if you are in hospital or too unwell or distressed to communicate.

Sadly there are situations where pregnancy loss is made more difficult by the reactions of others. That might include work colleagues being unsympathetic or your employer refusing to make accommodations to help you cope at work after loss. If this is happening to you, then you should keep notes about what is going on, get witnesses where possible, join and/or speak to your union, see Human Resources, or consult a lawyer. It may be more appropriate to seek other work rather than remain in a job that is not supporting you, although I know this option is often not open to many. SANDS has a guide for employers about creating supportive and respectful workplaces for those returning to work after loss www.sands.org.uk/sites/default/files/SANDS-INFO-EMPLOYERS.pdf.

Friends being critical about your loss or refusing to discuss what has gone on can be really painful. This may be due to them also coping with loss, or not knowing what to say. If it is a friendship you value you may want to tell them how you are feeling about your loss and what actions you need them to take to support you. For example, *'I am sure you mean well but your ideas about my loss really hurt me, I need you to listen and not judge'*, or *'I noticed you don't seem to want to talk about my miscarriage, has this affected you too? It would help me a lot if we can at least acknowledge it happened to me.'*

Chapter 7 (pp. 78–83)

Family may be subtly or overtly unkind about your loss, including directly holding you accountable or knowingly making cruel comments. In some cases family violence may happen in response to you losing a baby. As Chapter 7 outlines, partners can react in a variety of ways, which can seem indifferent, neglectful or hostile. While this can be due to them not knowing how to cope or managing their loss in self-destructive ways, there are situations where partners are deliberately abusive following loss. That commonly occurs where relationship violence was present before or during your pregnancy (and could even have contributed to your loss), or may happen after a miscarriage or stillbirth. Aggressive or abusive reactions are always difficult to bear and may feel almost impossible to cope with if you are also trying to come to terms with your loss or recover physically; or, if you are blaming yourself, may even accept abuse because you feel you deserve it.

Unfortunately pregnancy loss and domestic/relationship violence are linked, so do not panic if you are in an otherwise happy relationship or family situation and your doctor asks personal questions about abuse. They are just checking you are okay. If, however, you are at risk this is an opportunity to get help. If healthcare staff don't raise the issue then you can.

❝ When the midwife was examining me I started to cry. She was smart and asked if it was about the miscarriage or something else too. When I nodded she asked if all was okay at home. I shook my head. It was enough to alert her and with her help I was able to go to a refuge. ❞ Faye

We often wrongly assume that 'abuse' only counts if it involves serious physical violence. In fact abuse in relationships includes emotional abuse (cruel and belittling comments, gaslighting (deliberately making someone doubt themselves); undermining, jealousy and other controlling behaviour; financial abuse (withholding access to money); sexual abuse (unwanted sexual touching or assault); or physical violence (shoving, hitting, hair pulling, or threats to harm). Anyone can be affected, violence happens in all kinds of relationships and families – see this guide from UK Victim Support on recognizing the signs of abuse: www.victimsupport.org.uk/crime-info/types-crime/domestic-abuse/recognising-signs-domestic-abuse

If you are concerned about your own safety or a friend or family member you can get support via:

Refuge www.refuge.org.uk
Women's Aid www.womensaid.org.uk
National Coalition Against Domestic Violence (US) www.ncadv.org
National Domestic Violence Hotline (US) www.thehotline.org
Men's Advice Line www.mensadviceline.org.uk
Galop – the LGBT+ anti-violence charity www.galop.org.uk
SurvivorsUK: male rape and sexual abuse www.survivorsuk.org
National Association for People Abused in Childhood (NAPAC)
   https://napac.org.uk

Wikipedia has a list of international domestic violence helplines
https://en.wikipedia.org/wiki/List_of_domestic_violence_hotlines

You can also take the Freedom Programme www.freedomprogramme.co.uk,
a course that helps you understand and exit abuse, while preparing you to be
more confident in the future (including future relationships).

FURTHER HELP

Avert's resources on HIV and pregnancy
www.avert.org/learn-share/hiv-fact-sheets/pregnancy

The CDC's information on pregnancy and Zika
www.cdc.gov/zika/pregnancy

Genital herpes and pregnancy guide from the New Zealand
Herpes Foundation
www.herpes.org.nz/patient-info/herpes-pregnancy

NHS Rubella and pregnancy guide
www.nhs.uk/Livewell/Contraception/Documents/Rubella-pregnancy.
pdf

Malaria in Pregnancy Consortium
https://www.mip-consortium.org

NHS guide to toxoplasmosis during pregnancy
www.nhs.uk/common-health-questions/pregnancy/what-are-the-risks-
of-toxoplasmosis-during-pregnancy

Antenatal Results and Choices (ARC) guide to amniocentesis
www.arc-uk.org/tests-explained/amnio

Fibroid Network Online
www.fibroid.network

March of Dimes guide to Cervical Insufficiency and Short Cervix
www.marchofdimes.org/complications/cervical-insufficiency-and-
short-cervix.aspx

7. *The Needs and* FEELINGS OF PARTNERS

Partners remain the absent voices in conversations about pregnancy loss. They often want to talk about their experiences but can be sidelined and ignored by healthcare staff, families, and friends. Their main role is typically being the designated carer – offering physical and practical support during and after pregnancy loss, and acting as an intermediary between patient and healthcare staff; while relaying information to family and friends. If they have additional responsibilities for children or other dependents that will be balanced alongside these other roles. And they will be required to be 'the strong one'. This often translates as withholding feelings, not talking about their own grief or loss, or holding off talking about the loss(es) for fear of upsetting their partner.

A word about terminology

To recognize and respect how relationships and the people in them are diverse, 'Partner' here refers to anyone who is in a relationship with someone that has experienced a physical loss – including husbands, boyfriends, girlfriends, wives or significant others.

"I didn't know who to talk to"

HOW DO PARTNERS REACT
to pregnancy loss?

58%
STRUGGLE TO CONCENTRATE
finding it difficult to focus on everyday work, or even things they had previously enjoyed.

85%
SADNESS
often felt immediately after the loss, but for many partners these feelings continued for months or years afterwards – particularly if there were repeated losses, on significant anniversaries, or if they felt unable to comfort their loved one after loss.

47%
REPORTED SLEEP PROBLEMS
either not being able to get to sleep or waking early – and then thinking about their loss. Or feeling very sleepy during the day.

63%
GRIEF
that included being overwhelmed with sadness, crying, or feeling completely empty.

48%
SAID IT AFFECTED THEIR WORK
their energy, focus, concentration, patience, and motivation were all negatively affected.

58%
SHOCK
including feeling numb or disconnected, problems with concentration, anxiety and panic symptoms, or changes to sleep, appetite and concentration.

46%
DIDN'T SHARE ALL OF HOW THEY WERE FEELING WITH
their wife or girlfriend for fear of saying the wrong thing or causing further distress

22% DIDN'T TALK ABOUT ANY FEELINGS

of loss and pain with their partner.

22% OF PARTNERS FELT EXCLUDED BY HEALTHCARE STAFF

where staff were busy, focused on dealing with the physical symptoms of loss, or not having the time or skills to attend to partners.

38% WERE NOT OFFERED ADDITIONAL INFORMATION

about what was going on

63% SAID THEY WERE NOT TOLD OF ANY SUPPORT GROUPS OR SERVICES

for people who had experienced miscarriage, leaving them to either struggle alone, or seek out support online.

13% WERE DISTRESSED BY HOSPITAL COMMUNICATION

and worried by hospitals continuing to send letters about antenatal care after the loss.

[Source: 'Partners Too' survey completed by myself for the Miscarriage Association, July 2014. www.miscarriageassociation.org.uk/your-feelings/partners]

Common reactions to loss

Chapter 5
(pp. 53–57) You may be experiencing the same kinds of reactions as described in Chapter 5, and these may be acute during and after the loss. You may feel frightened and panicked by what is happening during a loss, especially if it is an emergency or you are the only person around to give assistance.

It is also common to be hit by very strong reactions some while after your loss. Partners have told me they often hid their feelings in going back to work, doing sport, or being busy in other ways – only to discover weeks or months later they were breaking down or unable to focus.

Other reactions you may identify with include:

Despair – this may be over the loss itself, fears about future fertility, or anxieties about how your relationship will survive.

Trauma – if you witnessed a loss you may struggle to process what happened or have repeated flashbacks or nightmares. That may be particularly acute if there was an emergency; if there was lots of blood or tissue; and if your partner was in a lot of pain, visibly distressed, or where their life was at risk.

66 *I really thought I had lost her. She was pale and hardly breathing.* 99 Simon

66 *I cannot get the sound of her screaming out of my head.* 99 Brandi

66 *I came home and cleaned the bathroom. I didn't want her to have to do that.* 99 Andrew

*"I thought I would lose her.
I really believed she was going to die"*

I have to be strong – this may be an overwhelming urge to protect and
care for your partner, or feeling this is your duty (other people may
put you in this role also). It may require such an emotional effort to
hold it together you may feel inside you are coming apart, you may find
yourself crying in private or become entirely numb as a way of getting
through.

Frustrated – wanting to do something to help or make it better but either
being uncertain what to do, not confident your actions will help, or
knowing there is nothing that can change the outcome of your loss.

Useless – watching a partner go through loss and seeing them in distress can leave you feeling helpless, worrying any care you offer is inadequate. It may be the first time in your life you have faced something there were not answers to, or you may have experienced losses before that you are reminded of:

66 *It's the one thing I've never been able to fix.* 99 Josh

66 *I can't make it better for her.* 99 Alison

66 *I want to give them a baby so much but so far I've failed to do that.* 99 Filip

66 *There wasn't a single thing I could do to stop it.* 99 Jonathan

"I felt hopeless. I didn't know how to help. I ended up redecorating the living room for something to do"

66 I just stood in the background while the doctors worked on her. 99 Mike

66 I didn't know what to say or do. 99 Donal

Wanting to take the pain away – when someone you love is in distress you obviously want to make it better for them:

66 I'd happily go through the physical pain to spare her from it. 99 Alex

66 I can hear her crying when she thinks I've gone to bed. It breaks my heart. 99 Ruby

66 I see other people with their babies and I know it hurts her every time. 99 Bako

Invisible – with so much going on and care mostly focused on the needs of the person having a physical loss, partners can feel they are not involved, or even welcome:

66 Nobody ever asked me if I was okay. 99 Kaspar

66 I might as well not have been there. 99 Will

66 I felt like a ghost. 99 Mohanned

"I felt helpless and shut out"

It's all my fault – blaming yourself for wanting a baby, helping your partner get pregnant, or if there have been arguments and disagreements (including over the pregnancy) you may feel like you were personally responsible for both the loss and any pain caused to your partner.

Did I cause this? – during and after loss you may be searching for meaning, unsure why the loss happened, or whether you could have spotted any warning signs or acted any sooner to prevent things going wrong. Noting you probably could not have known nor done anything to stop a loss may be comforting but you still may struggle to accept it.

Suspicion and uncertainty – you may be wondering why the loss happened and it may lead to unpleasant thoughts that your partner was somehow to blame for their miscarriage, ectopic pregnancy or stillbirth. Some partners have convinced themselves the loss happened because of past infidelity or an imagined affair, or due to having multiple past partners, drinking alcohol, using drugs or other behaviours. Often this is tied up with jealousy and may indicate a pre-existing problem with controlling behaviour you may wish to address with therapy (or, if you have been abusive to your partner previously or are concerned you may be in the future, to seek help from Respect http://respect.uk.net and consider leaving your relationship while you address your behaviour). Alternatively these reactions may be distressing if you have an otherwise positive relationship and if you feel guilty for having such strong reactions that are out of character.

How others may react to you

Family, friends, and workmates may surprise you if you let them know that you've had a loss. If you are sad, grieving or in shock it is a good idea to say so. Aside from it breaking the taboo of partners supposedly not caring or being so affected by loss, you may also discover others have felt just as you do and may be able to offer support and validation.

Sadly it is also common for friends and family or other people we're in contact with to either change the subject, not ask you how you are doing at all, or tell you how they think you should behave. You may find this includes telling you that your feelings are secondary, that you have no right to be upset, or that if you are distressed you should not speak of it.

When partners are assumed not to care

Where partners want to talk about pregnancy loss but cannot do so they may seem to others as if they are uncaring – either about the pregnancy loss or their loved one who has miscarried, had an ectopic pregnancy, or a stillbirth. This can lead to tensions and resentments. If you previously hid your feelings, you may want to explain this and note how you want to be more open. If you are not sure what to say or how to say it there are suggestions in The Pink Elephants Support Network's Partner Advice pinkelephantssupport.com/feel-home/support-resources/partner-brochure

I told her I'd been feeling sad the whole time. She never knew. She thought I wasn't bothered. When she realized I was we cried together and she said it made her feel so much better. Carly

Why do partners stay silent?

Here are the main reasons partners have shared with me for not feeling able to express themselves after loss:

- Don't want to cause more distress
- Scared of saying the wrong thing
- Family or friends advise them not to talk about it

- Nobody to listen (lack of support groups/services)
- No-one asked them
- Other people assume partners wouldn't be so upset
- Do not know what to say
- Afraid of breaking down

"I didn't want to add to her pain so I kept quiet about my feelings"

If you are not that bothered

As Chapters 5 and 6 indicate there are many ways to react to pregnancy loss and while most people are upset by their loss to a greater or lesser degree, not everyone is. Some partners talk about not being that upset and possibly feeling guilty for this. Or relieved the pregnancy is over – perhaps if they were unsure about parenthood or felt their relationship wasn't working. Still more partners are more focused on their loved one, wanting to be sure they recover and being relieved they survived if the loss was particularly traumatic and dangerous.

Connecting over your loss

There are different ways to express yourself and that may be in one conversation setting out how you feel, or lots of short discussions. It does not have to be formal, but can include:

- checking together how you both feel
- offering information about your reactions
- talking about what is happening
- identifying and using support services and further information (see Sources of support).

Sources of support (pp. 145–147)

You may also find the ideas in Chapter 8 about looking after yourself helpful to try alone or together. One of the biggest problems partners report is they did not know what to say, so starting from that can open up a conversation and let you either suggest ways of coping better together; or identifying what is needed to get and give love, care, and support.

Chapter 8 (pp. 88–93)

"We shared how we feel and comforted each other"

FURTHER HELP

The Father's Perspective in *Pregnancy After a Loss: A Guide to Pregnancy After a Miscarriage, Stillbirth, or Infant Death* (1999). Carol Cirulli Lanham. Berkley Books.

The Father's Experience in *A Silent Sorrow. Pregnancy Loss: Guidance and Support for You and Your Family* (2nd Ed) (2000). Ingrid Kohn and Perry-Lynn Moffitt. Routledge.

Vessels: A Love Story (2016). Daniel Raeburn. W.W. Norton.

Grieving Parents: Surviving Loss as a Couple (2014). Nathalie Himmelrich. Kat Biggie Press.

Partners Too – The Miscarriage Association
www.miscarriageassociation.org.uk/your-feelings/partners

Pink Families – lesbian and bisexual women's experiences of pregnancy loss

www.pinkfamilies.com/pregnancy-loss-lesbian-and-bisexual-womens-experience-of-loss

Australian Psychological Society *LGBT Pregnancy Loss*
https://psychology.org.au/for-the-public/Psychology-topics/LGBTI/LGBTI-Parenting/LGBT-Pregnancy-Loss

8. *Taking care*
OF YOU

This chapter focuses on ways to recover after loss.

Recovery is often discussed as something that is inspirational and dramatic. There is a crisis, we move past it, and life is good again. It allows for unhappy times, but not too many of them, and certainly not long term. In reality there is no upward path, clear stages to pass through, or a straightforward sense of 'getting better'. Instead you will have good days and bad days. If your pregnancy loss was particularly distressing it may take months or years to recover, and you may still find yourself troubled by aspects of your loss at unexpected moments. If you have recurrent miscarriages or infertility then you are unlikely to have just one loss to get over, instead there will be many losses and subsequent difficult life decisions to make.

YOUR RECOVERY IS GOING TO BE AFFECTED BY

- what your circumstances were like prior to your loss
- what happened physically during your miscarriage, ectopic pregnancy, or stillbirth
- how you and your partner coped during and immediately after your loss
- whether you had help or hindrance from friends, family, your community, or work colleagues
- if your health care was well or poorly delivered
- whether you have experienced losses before
- if you have fertility problems
- if there are other life events affecting you (e.g. financial, housing, or relationship difficulties)
- if you are an older parent

Or if you are dealing with pre-existing stigma, prejudice or other barriers where healthcare and support services are not accessible or welcoming and wider structural barriers, isolation, and prejudice make everything a struggle. Particularly if you are in one or more of these groups:

- unemployed, on a low income, or living in poverty
- a very young parent
- a single parent
- disabled or have a chronic illness
- Black, Indigenous, a Person of Colour, or a Gypsy or Traveller
- are LGBT.

Ways of coping

Hearing from other people who've been there – reading stories about other people's losses, browsing conversations in online forums and support groups, or talking to friends or family members that have also experienced loss can remind you that you are not alone.

> ❝ *I thought I would cry forever. I couldn't stop. My sister reminded me when she had her ectopic pregnancy she was the same. I remember her seeming so strong but she said she didn't feel that way. She said it was important to let myself be sad for as long as I needed.* ❞ Neave

Talking it over – there may be several aspects or just one part of your loss you wish to focus on. That could include discussing what happened when you miscarried, questions or concerns about your loss that are unanswered, or giving voice to all your feelings. You can talk to your partner, friends or family, or support groups, helplines, or healthcare staff.

Creative expressions – you may want to document how you feel in letters to yourself or to your partner or your baby; in poetry or short stories; keeping a diary, or using crafting; photography or film to record how you feel, provide an outlet for your emotions, or act as a distraction (see Chapter 13).

Chapter 13
(pp. 133–136)

New hobbies and interests – if you cannot stop thinking about your loss and it is taking over, you may want to channel your energies into other activities. This could include sport and exercise, dance, social or book clubs, or volunteering. Some people use this as a form of physical recovery and feeling stronger, while others use it to stop intrusive thoughts, and still more to memorialize their loss (see Chapter 13).

Chapter 13
(pp. 133–141)

Setting yourself goals and targets

While you may need time to rest and come to terms with your loss, there will be things you need to do as part of daily life. That may include caring for existing children and pets, going to work, housework and daily chores, personal care, and socializing.

Doing this may be difficult if you are still processing trauma, or experiencing physical or psychological symptoms. You can build in systems to motivate yourself, even if you do not feel like doing much. Setting yourself daily goals is useful and it may help to write these down, put them in your phone, or set reminders in your diary:

> *Today I have to* – note any essential things that have to be done, see if any can be put off or delegated to someone else. If you have any control over events in your day start with things you like the most or are easy to achieve; this may help build momentum to keep going and stop you feeling overwhelmed.

> *Today I want to* – these are things that make you feel positive or you are unsure if you are able to do but would like to try.

Having just one essential thing to do, even if it's get out of bed and have a cup of tea, may leave you feeling capable of doing more – and accepting if today is not one of those days.

POSITIVE THINGS I CAN DO FOR MYSELF TODAY

Make myself a hot drink

Have a shower or bath

Read a book

Listen to music

Phone a friend

Look at pictures on Instagram

Take my dog for a walk

Share a meal with friends or family

Remind myself how well I am doing

Suggestions for self-care and comfort

The following exercises can require a little practice, but may be calming and soothing.

Catching your breath

If you are in crisis you may struggle to breathe, or feel as if you are drowning or suffocating. Recognising these are symptoms of shock and panic and actively changing how you breathe can have powerful results. You can do this with breathing exercises – concentrating on counting how long you are inhaling, holding and exhaling for; while noting how your breath sounds as it goes out and in. Some people also visualize breathing in kindness, confidence or love and breathing out pain and despair. There are a number of variations on this exercise. Some people like breathing in, holding and out for the same number of seconds (e.g. in for 4, hold for 4, out for 4). While others prefer in for 4, hold for 7 out for 8 (called the 4, 7, 8 method). You can work out which is most comfortable for you.

Mindfulness, meditation, and relaxation techniques

While sitting or lying, focus on your toes, wriggling them and tensing them before relaxing, moving on up through your body through calves, knees, thighs, stomach, chest, fingers, hands, arms, and finally your neck and face. You can also repeat this in descending order. If you have numbness or lack of feeling due to paralysis or nerve damage, or are limbless or an amputee, you may wish to focus on parts of the body where you do have sensation. This is a gentle exercise not physical activity so if anything hurts then stop and try another time.

Or try the 'warm jelly' exercise. As before you begin at your feet and imagine you are slowly being filled with warm, orange jelly. It moves up through your body until you feel weighed down by it. After holding that feeling for a short time you imagine all the jelly running out from your toes, emptying through your body and carrying any sadness or negative emotions you have with it. If you don't like the idea of jelly then warm sand, or imagining you are being filled with sunlight, might be a good alternative.

Other relaxation activites are available from:
Moodjuice www.moodjuice.scot.nhs.uk/relaxation.asp
Downloadable self-help guides www.moodjuice.scot.nhs.uk/asppodcast.asp
Free Mindfulness project www.freemindfulness.org/download

Mindfulness is a technique to help you feel stronger emotionally and better able to enjoy and engage with life. While it has its roots in Buddhism, you can be any religion or none and still use it. Put simply it means focusing on what is going on around you right now (in your mind, body, and immediate surroundings). It can allow you to be aware of how you are thinking or feeling (physically or emotionally); note unhelpful or destructive thoughts; feel calmer and reduce panic; and build emotional resilience.

During mindfulness exercises you might pause, sit or lie down and (as described above) note your surroundings, pay attention to your breathing, and also any thoughts that come into your mind. It may be you don't think of anything, or all kinds of thoughts come to you. As they do, let them in, note them without an attempt to develop, fix, or pass judgement. You are simply observing what occurs during the time you are doing this exercise (people find a couple of minutes is good at first, building to 5, 10 or 15 minutes). At the end of this exercise take a moment to think about what was in your head (if anything). It might be something you decide to leave behind, or come back to. Following loss you may find this unsettling, or very helpful if your head is racing or you are overwhelmed with many strong emotions but you do not feel able to make any real sense of what they mean.

Instructions on how to practise mindfulness can be found at:

Be Mindful http://bemindful.co.uk
Moodjuice www.moodjuice.scot.nhs.uk/mildmoderate/MindfulnessDown loads.asp
Breathworks www.breathworks-mindfulness.org.uk/online-courses (they offer taster sessions to see if this is something that works for you)
Headspace www.headspace.com/register (offers a free trial before you commit to the course)

Lots of parents are drawn to candle meditation after loss. Aside from lighting candles being associated with remembrance, having an area of your home where you keep a candle you may light either to be a reminder of your baby or a specific focal point may be reassuring. For the candle meditation, light a candle (you can do this in a light or dark room but many find a darkened room is more effective). Sit comfortably, facing the candle and begin to watch it. It may take some practice to keep focused on the candle and you may find your gaze moves away, every time it does just bring it back to the candle. Notice the size of the flame, the colour, how it moves. It might help you to focus your feelings into the candle, thinking positive thoughts of your baby or imagine letting the light of the candle help you feel warmer inside. Repeating this over time may allow you to build up the amount of time you wish to spend on the exercise. Some people find this something they can share with a partner, both sitting together looking at the candle flame, sharing a quiet moment of concentration purely on the light in front of them, or silent reflection about the baby you have lost.

The idea of these activities is not to worsen or revisit trauma, so if you find yourself struggling during or after or experiencing nightmares or other distressing thoughts stop, and speak to your doctor and/or therapist. It is worth noting if you are particularly unwell mentally these are not appropriate and are unlikely to work or be something you can manage.

Chapter 4 (pp. 40–43)

Recovery isn't just about trying to get pregnant again

Getting over a miscarriage, ectopic pregnancy or stillbirth is often presented solely as preparing for another pregnancy as quickly as possible. Indeed this used to be standard advice. However it assumed everyone will be able to do this – or wants to. It may be much more helpful if you focus on recovering physically and mentally after loss so you feel stronger within your body and mind.

MY FIRST AID KIT

- time to be alone and compose myself (for example the bathroom at work, or going for a walk)
- having tissues, mints, makeup, handwipes etc. to freshen up after crying
- creating something that calms or distracts – a novel, colouring book, a piece of music to listen to, or a saying I've devised for myself to repeat in my head until I feel able to focus again
- someone I can call or see if I feel the need to offload (partner, friend, or support group helpline)

Recovery is not forgetting

A big barrier to recovery is a fear that if you 'get better' you will forget. While a physically or psychologically painful loss may be tough to move on from, you may also have a belief that holding onto the pain is also a means of staying connected with your baby (or babies). You may feel guilty for having good days or even days where you haven't thought about your loss or been happy or distracted. Getting over your loss is not disloyal. It is not about pretending you were not pregnant or your loss was not important. It does not mean you didn't love your baby or indicate anything about your ability to be a good parent. All it means is you are doing better psychologically and physically. There are plenty of ways you can remember and mark your loss (see Chapter 13) and you may find if you are stronger emotionally and physically you'll also be in a better position to memorialize, try again to conceive, or decide not to get pregnant (see Chapter 11).

Chapter 13
(pp. 132–137)

Chapter 11
(pp. 109–117)

FURTHER HELP

Healing Your Grieving Heart After Stillbirth: 100 Practical Ideas for Parents and Families, Compassionate Advice and Simple Activities to Help You Through Your Grief (2013). Alan D. Wolfelt and Raelynn Maloney. Companion Books.

Empty Cradle, Broken Heart: Surviving the Death of Your Baby (3rd Ed) (2016). Deborah L. Davis. Fulcrum.

Stillbirth, Yet Still Born: Grieving and Honoring Your Precious Baby (2014). Deborah L. Davis. Fulcrum.

8 Keys to Safe Trauma Recovery: Take-charge Strategies to Empower Your Healing (2010). Babette Rothschild. W. W. Norton and Co.

OTHER PEOPLE'S STORIES OF LOSS AND RECOVERY

Dead Babies and Seaside Towns (2017). Alice Jolly. Unbound.

Eye of the Storm: The Silent Grief of Miscarriage (2016). Rachel McGrath. McGrath House. See also www.findingtherainbow.net

Miscarriage Matters to Mothers: The Book of Stories (Vol. 1) (2014). Michelle L. Myers. CreateSpace Independent Publishing Platform.

Dare to Dream: My Struggle to Become a Mum – A Story of Heartache and Hope (2017). Izzy Judd. Bantam Press. Also has updates on Instagram on fertility, pregnancy, parenthood, and loss topics (www.instagram.com/mrs_izzyjudd) as does Giovanna Fletcher (www.instagram.com/mrsgifletcher).

The Legacy of Leo – https://thelegacyofleo.com (also includes support and information for LGBT parents).

Life after baby loss: a companion and guide for parents. Nicola Gaskin (2018) (plus updates on Instagram www.instagram.com/onedayofwinter).

Surviving My First Year Of Child Loss: Personal Stories From Grieving Parents (2017). Nathalie Himmelrich. Reach for the Sky.

9. *Looking Out*
FOR YOUR RELATIONSHIP

Dealing with pregnancy loss can strengthen some relationships particularly if you have been able to communicate clearly and grieve in similar ways. You may find you feel emotionally close, share more physical affection, and are able to focus on the positive aspects of your life.

However, pregnancy loss can also cause relationship strain or breakdown – either because there were problems in the relationship prior to pregnancy loss; due to the stress of coping with past losses; or because there is a disconnect in how you both cope with the loss leading to rifts, disagreements, and resentments. Even the strongest and happiest relationships can struggle when put under pressure – and the shock and trauma some people experience during and after loss can cause difficulties even if you very much want to stay together.

Being afraid your relationship could be adversely affected by pregnancy loss can also make coping with miscarriage more difficult. You may experience more arguments; find yourself disagreeing over silly things that ordinarily would not bother you; blaming; shutting each other out; or disagreeing about the best ways to cope or what to do next. In particular there may be tensions if one of you wants to try again to get pregnant and the other does not; if you cannot agree on further support for fertility worries; or where you are unwilling or unable to meet each other's emotional needs.

Ways to connect during and after loss

Sometimes people are afraid to talk together about their pregnancy loss for fear it will either upset them more, or distress their partner. However, if anything about your loss is troubling you (whether it happened recently or in the past), it is better to tell your partner how you feel. Connecting can be:

Verbal – you talk over how you feel, remember positive things about your relationship, ask about what is going on, discuss what has happened during the loss and future care needs (if appropriate), and reflect on whether or not you want to try again.

Physical – hugging, holding hands, showering or bathing together, massage, or other ways of being connected that you both enjoy.

Practical – doing things together you like. Cooking for each other and sharing meals, watching a film, having a holiday, taking up a hobby, DIY, or taking on additional chores.

Acts of kindness – finding something positive online to share, picking a meaningful song, or buying a bunch of flowers. Thinking about little ways to show one another you are on each other's mind does not have to be expensive but can feel reassuring.

❝ As I was leaving hospital my nurse said to me 'Fit your own lifejacket first'. I asked her what she meant and she explained I needed to take care of myself before caring for anyone else. It was useful to remind me not to jump back into everyday life and to keep checking what I needed, especially on days when I felt stressed, down or that I was getting worse, not better. ❞ **Hannah**

Everyone is different, some prefer to express themselves by words, touch or deeds; but if you were not keen on these prior to your pregnancy loss it may feel uncomfortable or artificial. However, it is a good idea to note if one of you would like to connect in a particular way and the other isn't aware of this to share what you need.

I could do with a hug.
Can you listen while I share how I feel?
I'm exhausted, can you cook dinner tonight please?

We often assume we know what to do during a crisis, or that our partner should be aware of our needs and act accordingly. Resentments can be reduced if you are specific about the help you need – and it allows for you to get additional support if one of you can't offer the other care. Thinking about what you are asking for is a good idea, as if your partner is obviously grieving but you also need emotional support you may wish to get additional help from support groups or a therapist rather than expecting them to attend to you if they really are not up to it.

Communication strategies

We all express ourselves in different ways, but here are some key strategies people that have been through pregnancy loss have told me helped their relationships:

Listen – allow each other to talk about feelings, fears, hopes and other emotions.

Don't interrupt – let each other speak without talking over each other or telling each other how to think and feel.

Start a conversation – it may be that you have wanted to say something for a while but have not felt able to, or sense your partner wishes to talk. Or you may just decide it is good idea to find out how you both are doing. Opening up a dialogue may be the trickiest part, but other people have found saying things like:
I notice you've been sad, can you tell me how you are doing?
I've been thinking about our baby and wondered if you had too.
Can I tell you about how I feel?
Your check-up is tomorrow, do you want me to come with you? Is there anything we need to prepare before you see the doctor?

Find a place to talk – that may be at home during the evening when you aren't going to be interrupted, over a meal, while on a break or holiday, at a set time, or just informally as you feel the need. Some people like to know there is an end to the conversation so pick a car journey or a walk in the park that they know will finish and stop the discussion.

Sources of support (pp. 145–147)

Find a means to communicate that suits you – which might include expressing yourself in email, letters, phone, in person, finding films or songs that explain how you feel. Several of the charities listed in Sources of support have poems, writing, films, photographs and cartoons where other people who have experienced pregnancy loss are sharing their stories – if they resonate with yours but you don't feel able to express yourself you could direct your partner to reading them instead.

Don't expect to fix things – when someone we love is distressed, anxious, angry or uncertain we may want to reassure them, calm them down, or help them feel better. While you do not want to ignore someone who is upset, resist the temptation to tell them it is okay, will be better soon, or how you feel they should be thinking or feeling. Not all of this can be fixed and listening may be better (see above).

Don't change subject or move on – if your partner is trying to tell you how they feel then listen. If it is too upsetting for you, it is okay to be honest about this and suggest you discuss it later while noting you care about them and don't want them to be distressed.

There is no correct or set timescale – it is normal to be upset weeks or months after a loss so do not expect a swift recovery or be irritated if one or both of you needs time to recoup.

Phrases people have found useful when trying to navigate emotional and sensitive conversations include:

I want to help but I need you to let me know how I can best support you.
I know you need to share the details but I'm finding that really difficult to hear, can you talk about that with the doctor? It doesn't mean I don't love you nor care about our loss.
I don't know the answers either, shall we try and find out some together?
I messed up, I want to try again and talk this over, it's important.
Help me out here.
I don't know what to do.
I would like to talk, but not right now.
I really am okay, I don't need anything but if you do I will listen.

Therapy or mediation can be a bonus if you are struggling to communicate or feel there are barriers between you. If you feel the need to talk a lot about what has happened it is a good idea to share how you feel with others. Particularly if one of you wishes to talk more, or one or both of you find going over what happened or thinking about the future is traumatic. It is not disloyal or wrong to talk to other people – trusted friends or family members or using other services such as charities, or support groups (see Sources of support).

Sources
of support
(pp. 145–147)

Emotionally fraught conversations can mean we act in ways that are moody, aggressive, or spiteful. We may want to express all kinds of angry and unpleasant emotions that may feel scary to say and hear. Being able to vent in this way is better than bottling up feelings, but you may discover it is difficult or unacceptable to do so – based on your gender, culture or other factors. If you do not feel safe sharing, then writing how you feel or using support services may be sensible. Noting also that reacting strongly to your loss does not mean you do not care about your partner or existing children; nor the baby you lost. It may help you to clarify "*I am angry* – but not with you".

"I can't bear seeing other families with babies"

Disagreements and difficulties following loss may be difficult to forgive and forget – but they do happen and being able to accept this is common, sad, but not automatically a sign there is a crisis in your relationship is sensible. Finding other ways to share affection (see above) may aid recovery. If, however, your relationship is abusive ongoing unkindness may be a 'red flag' worth heeding (see Chapter 6).

Chapter 6
(pp. 73–74)

When to seek other support

Therapy might include you seeing a counselor alone, together, or with other people that have been through similar experiences. The therapist may focus specifically on your loss and overcoming trauma; or they may wish to help you prepare for the future (trying again, considering future testing and treatment, or deciding to stop trying); or if your current issues in dealing with loss are tied up in past problems they may wish to address all of those issues.

Therapy sessions are time-limited (usually 40 minutes to one hour) and repeated over a set period of time (usually weeks but possibly months). The therapist will ask all about what happened and set targets with you about what you want to get from therapy. If you are on a low income many therapists offer a sliding scale or local charities may have some therapy available. Support groups may also be very valuable if you need someone to listen and talk to.

Some therapists will offer you 'homework' – activities to try or resources to read in between therapy sessions that you feed back on. Some therapy is directive and structured, others less so. It is a good idea to call a few therapists first to find one you feel able to open up to, and who is experienced in working with people who have had miscarriage, ectopic pregnancy, and stillbirth. You should also check your therapist is confident in dealing with diversity if you are disabled; Lesbian, a Bisexual Woman or Transgender; a Black, Indigenous, Person of Colour, Gypsy or Traveller; or if you are a young parent – as you do not wish any issues with your loss worsened by a therapist that is not fully prepared to understand and support your specific needs.

Therapists are not there to take sides, check for lying or deceit, tell you what to do, or fix things for you. Couples therapy is also not advised if you are in an abusive relationship (although individual therapy may be an excellent idea if you are wanting to exit an abusive relationship and are recovering after loss). Chapter 6 (pp. 73–74)

More information on how to pick a therapist, what to expect in therapy, and what will happen in your first therapy session at: www.bacp.co.uk/about-therapy/how-to-get-therapy

If your relationship ends

Relationships can break down at any point, and while some end after pregnancy loss it does not mean the loss caused the separation. It may have made things more difficult, or brought to the fore other problems within the relationship. Or it could be the relationship ends for unrelated reasons. Deciding to separate is rarely easy and you may opt to have some time apart to focus on what you want to do. You may also wish to use therapy to work out if you wish to stay together or part, and if the relationship is to end to manage this as well as you are able (particularly if you have children). Or you may wish to use therapy for yourself to cope with a separation.

It may be neglect, blame, or a lack of compassion during and after loss mean you no longer wish to be together. Or you cannot move past what you went through and now want a new start. Knowing you have been through loss can make it more difficult to separate as you may feel there is a shared history, or you do not want to hurt each other more than has already happened. However, staying together just because you had a loss or out of a sense of duty or guilt is not a good idea.

If you feel the relationship is over the following organisations and resources may be helpful:

Family Lives www.familylives.org.uk
Separated Families www.separatedfamilies.info
National Family Mediation www.nfm.org.uk

If you are single

Not everyone is in a relationship at the time of pregnancy loss. You may have got pregnant by choice or accident while dating but not be currently together. Or it may be your relationship ended during the pregnancy, or before or after the loss. If you were not involved with the person who got you pregnant then you may need friends or family to help you – assuming they are supportive. In some cases those around you who were judgemental about the pregnancy may be equally unpleasant about your loss, making tactless comments about it being for the best or suggesting it was somehow punishment for getting pregnant to begin with. This may be more of an issue for you if you are a young woman.

Whether you're single or in a relationship the Miscarriage Association have specific resources for you if you are a young person who has experienced pregnancy loss www.miscarriageassociation.org.uk/your-feelings/young-people.

Should I tell them about the loss?

If you were not together before the loss, or had split up, then it is your choice whether to share details of what has happened. If they were aware you were pregnant you may wish to tell them you had experienced pregnancy loss – assuming they will not be dismissive or unpleasant about it. If they were not aware you may want them to know you were pregnant and lost your baby, although this may be difficult if you, or they, feel you are doing this to upset them or get them into a relationship with you. If you do not feel up to sharing your news presently you can always tell them in the future.

Grieving together, while apart

Even if your relationship is over, both of you may feel sad about the loss. You may not want to be together but both of you have a loss to grieve. Or it may be you are distressed both by the relationship ending and pregnancy loss – particularly if you had hoped the baby would at least have kept you in each other's lives.

It can be confusing after loss where you have strong emotions and a desire to support someone you care for even if you are no longer together. Some people find themselves reuniting after loss – temporarily or permanently. Others struggle to set clear boundaries or manage their emotions.

Being clear what you want and can offer is important – so noting the relationship is over but you can still help practically with shopping, or talking about your loss, or memorializing (see Chapter 13) may be better than giving one or both of you false hope.

Chapter 13
(pp. 133–136)

Single and using Assisted Conception

If you used assisted conception to get pregnant, are single, and have had a loss you may feel very alone. Drawing on the support of friends, family, healthcare staff and help groups may be a good idea. You may need time off work, and help in looking after yourself as you recover physically and emotionally.

Relationships after loss

Whether you were single or your relationship broke down, dating after loss can be a source of hope, or stress (or both). You may be anxious about having sex again or future pregnancy. The ideas in Chapter 11 on trying again may be reassuring to focus on pleasure, redefining what intimacy may mean to you, and thinking about contraception. You may feel very strongly you want to get pregnant again, and that may be something you try and do either with assisted conception or with a new partner. Talking through these understandable desires is a good idea so you do not risk either trying before you are physically ready or begin a pregnancy with someone who is not fully aware of your desires and isn't able to consent to parenthood.

Chapter 11
(pp. 109–117)

FURTHER HELP

RELATIONSHIP ADVICE

5 Love Languages www.5lovelanguages.com

Mating in Captivity (2007). Esther Perel. Hodder and Stoughton.

DATING ADVICE

Flirt Coach (2009). Peta Heskell. Thorsons.

Be Your Own Love Coach: Ways to Help You Find and Keep Your Soulmate (2005). Ariana Gee and Mary Gregory. New Holland Publishers.

Jean Smith: Flirtology https://flirtology.com

10. *Moving*
FORWARD

Life continues after loss, and you may find that easier or more difficult than anticipated. This chapter explores what to expect from being in the wider world while recovering after pregnancy loss.

Removing stressors

You may want to carry out a 'life check' noting all the things that might cause you additional stress that right now you do not need to deal with. Things other people who've experienced pregnancy loss have tackled include:

Work – either cutting back on their work hours, changing jobs, having some time off as sick/compassionate leave, or speaking to their boss/HR/union if there are existing work problems you need help with.

Finances – if you are worried about money then taking advice from the organisations listed in Chapter 5 may help you feel less stressed. You can also speak to your doctor if physically or mentally you are unable to work but this is impacting on your financial situation.

Chapter 5
(p. 58)

Family difficulties – if you have problems with relatives or existing children this can be exacerbated if you are either trying to come to terms with loss, or where you are being treated unkindly or unsympathetically (see Chapter 6). The following charities can help those who are struggling to cope both with pregnancy loss and difficult family circumstances:

Chapter 6
(pp. 71–74)

Family Lives www.familylives.org.uk
Stand Alone http://standalone.org.uk
Home Start www.home-start.org.uk

Relationship problems – trying to overcome relationship difficulties or agreeing to part may be necessary during or after loss – see Chapter 9.

Chapter 9
(pp. 101–102)

For some people pregnancy loss can be hugely disruptive and lead them to reevaluate their lives as a consequence. Other people do not make major changes or plans and largely carry on as before their loss. You should only worry if you are making dramatic, out of character, and self-destructive life choices.

When everyone seems pregnant but you

Dealing with pregnancy loss can be far harder when you have to interact with other friends, workmates or family members that are pregnant or have new babies or young children. While you may be happy for them, you may also feel empty, angry, resentful or afraid for your future. Noting this is most likely going to be unavoidable, and considering how you are going to respond may let you feel more in control than panicking every time you have to talk to someone pregnant or who has a newborn or child.

There are a number of ways you can cope. Some people accept while they have had a loss, they bear no ill will to others who have managed to get pregnant or have a baby, they continue to see and celebrate with them as they always have done. It does not mean they hide any upset this causes, but they vent about it in private.

Alternatively you may prefer to be upfront with friends or family members that you don't feel able to be around them when you have just experienced a loss. Most people are aware that talking about their pregnancies or new babies can be insensitive and so avoid this topic, but where this doesn't happen and if it upsets you then you have every right to ask them if you could discuss something else. You might prefer to keep in touch via phone, skype or email or on social media rather than meeting in person.

Equally you may be okay about other people being pregnant or having a newborn, but their discomfort around you following loss can be really hard. You can tell people if you want to be near them and that it is fine for them to involve you in their pregnancy or parenthood. This may be particularly the case where you have been pregnant but people act as if you haven't been, or where you have names for your baby and want to talk about them but other people change the subject.

> 66 *Her name is Tiana. It is okay to say it. She will always be my baby.* 99 **Karen**

Anticipating Triggers

As you recover from your loss(es) you can expect some days to be easier than others. Particular events may also be harder to deal with – for example family gatherings, festivals, parties, remembrance weeks, or occasions like Mother's or Father's day. The dates when you got pregnant, experienced your loss(es) or what would have been due dates may also be difficult. Some people opt to avoid these occasions immediately after their loss, or perhaps indefinitely. Others are able to mark them or just ignore them. Noting when potential triggers might arise allows you to calm and prepare yourself and create strategies where you can feel comforted and safe. Sometimes film and TV storylines, a song on the radio, or someone mentioning your (or their) loss can catch you by surprise, so using your strategies from Chapter 8 will help you feel better in control.

Chapter 8
(pp. 87–94)

Dealing with loneliness and isolation

After loss you may feel like other people cannot understand what you have gone through, or even if you recognize you are not unique in experiencing loss you still feel that you are on your own. These feelings are normal and often part of the grieving process, and sometimes you may feel sad about not having other people to talk to you may still not really feel like opening up about your loss. Giving yourself time and working out how and when you want to connect with other people is a good idea.

Some options other people have found useful include:

- Calling a helpline
- Joining a support group (in person or virtually)
- Asking friends or family members you can trust to be there for you
- Joining a social club or hobby group that has nothing to do with pregnancy loss, but where you can feel you're in good company

You might also find the ideas in the Loneliness Resource Pack (www.jrf.org. uk/report/loneliness-resource-pack) helpful, or applying the ideas you put in

Chapter 8 (p. 94) your personal first aid kit (see Chapter 8).

11. *Deciding to*
TRY AGAIN
(OR NOT)

It is entirely your decision whether or not to try again to get pregnant, and when you want to do that (noting if you used assisted conception your choices may not be straightforward). You may not be up to considering this right now, or your main goal may be to try to conceive again as quickly as possible. Alternatively you may not be sure what to do.

In the past, advice from doctors was always to try again as swiftly as possible, with the mistaken belief that another pregnancy and, hopefully, a new baby, would distract from a past loss. While this can work for some people, it ignores that not everyone that experiences miscarriage, ectopic pregnancy or stillbirth gets pregnant again quickly, or stays pregnant. Future pregnancy losses can still happen. Anxieties about being pregnant after loss (see Chapter 12) are common. And being pregnant or having a new baby may not mean you forget about past losses (nor want to).

Chapter 12
(p. 123)

Trying again may be affected by your age, the quality of your relationship, your mental and physical health, your financial situation, and fertility issues.

This chapter covers different options you may have around trying again. This might include:

- doing absolutely nothing right now, and seeing in the future how you feel about having sex and trying to conceive
- agreeing together you want to try and conceive quickly and to resume having sex and/or fertility treatment
- noting that in the future you would like to try and get pregnant again, but right now it is not a priority or something you feel ready to try
- seeking medical help and/or fertility advice if you are worried about your mental or physical health, have had recurrent losses, or found it difficult to conceive
- decide to stop trying.

You can have sex whether or not you are planning to get pregnant (in whatever way you intend to conceive) as that can feel healing, connecting, comforting and enjoyable. But equally you may not want any kind of intimacy in the weeks or months after loss.

Questions to ask yourself before trying again after loss

Am I healthy physically (including recovery from surgery or infection)?
Do I/we need to have any further medical tests or monitoring?
How likely is it that I might experience another loss?
Do I have support if there is an increased risk of loss or high-risk pregnancy?
How am I doing psychologically?
How might we cope with another pregnancy, or another loss?
Is our relationship okay?
What are our reasons for getting pregnant again (for example, do I want to replace the baby I lost)?

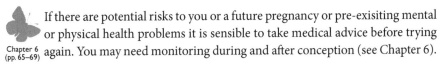

If there are potential risks to you or a future pregnancy or pre-exisiting mental or physical health problems it is sensible to take medical advice before trying Chapter 6 (pp. 65–69) again. You may need monitoring during and after conception (see Chapter 6).

Your feelings about trying again

People's reactions to trying again vary. Here are the most common responses people have told me they have felt:

Hopeful – they may or may not be ready to try and conceive right now, but they feel this is something possible for the future and believe they can cope whether or not they get pregnant again.

Anxious – where people are either troubled by their past loss, or are concerned they either will not get pregnant again or will miscarry in subsequent pregnancies. They may also be worried about other aspects of their life going wrong because of pregnancy loss.

Guilty – this might be over past loss, or wondering if it is disloyal or disrespectful to try again.

Fearful – similar to anxiety, people can be very frightened by what happened physically and emotionally during and after pregnancy loss; or scared they may cause future losses; or risk losing their relationship if they cannot have a baby.

Certain and Optimistic – in some cases people say they simply 'just know' they will get pregnant again and are not concerned about future losses.

Demoralized – whether there has been one or many losses, people may feel exhausted by the thought of having to try again, to face future miscarriages, or to seek further medical help (particularly if past care has been time consuming, expensive, and invasive).

Unsure – this may include being uncertain about why previous losses happened, undecided over whether to try again or not, or worried about future losses or fertility.

Ready – in some cases there is no room for thinking about what is going on, people say inside they just feel ready to try again, that may be a general sense of wanting to get pregnant or an overwhelming urge to conceive.

While you are considering your options you may find this leaflet from the Miscarriage Association reassuring: *Thinking About Another Pregnancy* www.miscarriageassociation.org.uk/your-feelings/thinking-about-another-pregnancy

Questions and concerns about trying again

When should we try?

Advice about trying to get pregnant after loss varies. The World Health Organization suggests 6 months after miscarriage before trying again, while most western physicians are trained to advise a 3 month wait. Aside from giving people space to recover physically and emotionally, a gap between pregnancy loss and future pregnancies was believed to reduce the chance of future miscarriage, pre-eclampsia, preterm births, or gestational diabetes. But recent medical evidence suggests so long as there are no other complications or physical health issues you can try again as soon as you feel like it, noting no differences in adverse outcomes whether people try again after 3 months (or sooner) or wait longer.

If you are physically and emotionally ready to try again this may be good news. However, if you are not yet psychologically prepared to conceive or still grieving your loss you should not feel pressured to try before you are up to it. And your doctor may advise you to wait if you are medicated for infection after loss (or any miscarriage treatment, see Chapter 3); if you have had an ectopic pregnancy and taking methotrexate; following a molar pregnancy; or if you have had recurrent miscarriages that are being explored.

Chapter 3 (pp. 21–26)

Some people have a personal preference based not on time but on physical recovery – so putting off receiving oral and penetrative sex and trying to conceive until they have stopped bleeding, or have had a period.

Is it disloyal to try again?

Mourning your miscarriage or stillbirth may leave you feeling that trying again means forgetting the baby you lost. Your previous pregnancies and losses will always count in ways that are meaningful to you. A future pregnancy will not be a replacement. If you are still feeling distressed or too guilty to try again then it may be better to wait, and consider the support of preg-

Sources of support
(pp. 145–147)

nancy loss groups (see Sources of support) or therapy. Deciding to try again can feel like moving on in positive ways, or more bittersweet. You may want to memorialize your baby if you have not had a way to say goodbye and feel this might help you mark a shift between a loss and trying to conceive (see

Chapter 13
(pp. 133–141)

Chapter 13). It is not disloyal or unfair to try again.

What if there is another miscarriage?

Having experienced one or more losses, you may feel anxious future pregnancies may end in miscarriage or stillbirth. And that is a possibility. If you are afraid about the physical or emotional aspects of loss or are still coming to terms with the grief and trauma of your last one, then waiting or seeking support and therapy may help you weigh up your options and approach trying to conceive in a confident yet pragmatic way. Some people decide to try again, accepting they may not get or stay pregnant. Others choose to stop trying if past loss(es) were hard to bear, or understand if medical investigations reveal there is little or no hope of getting or staying pregnant. Or you may continue to try again even if you do not feel completely recovered. This may be particularly the case if you are concerned that waiting is going to be detrimental to your ability to conceive (for example older parents, or those using assisted conception).

What if I cannot get pregnant?

If you have had several miscarriages or have struggled to conceive, thinking about trying again can feel stressful. Discussing with your doctor, having medical and fertility investigations, and seeing a counsellor that specializes in fertility problems may give you better insights into your situation, additional options (see below) and whether to try again. Some people continue to try even if they feel there is little hope, others prefer to enjoy intimacy (see below) without intending to get pregnant.

When you want to try again very quickly

Feeling driven to have sex after loss is a taboo topic, but certainly very common. The desire to feel close to another person is understandable while coping with grief and trauma. When we talk about 'trying again' or 'trying to conceive' this may gloss over how intimacy may also serve to distract us from a loss or enable us to feel more connected and united. Pleasure, too, may be important, although you may feel uncertain if this is appropriate. Answer: it is if it brings you comfort and helps you feel better.

When you want to wait

If you do not want to get pregnant, or have been advised to postpone getting pregnant, or where you are using fertility treatments, you may still wish to experience intimacy. For some people this may be exploring ways to get and give pleasure (see below), for others they may prefer to avoid any kind of sexual activity for a while. It is okay to explore intimacy if you want to, accepting you are not trying to get pregnant at this time. If you need to use contraception, considering your choices (see below) allows you to focus on experiencing pleasure when you want it without having to think about pregnancy. Remember, forcing yourself to have sex when you don't want to may be bad for your mental health, just as beating yourself up mentally for not trying before you feel ready can be.

Contraception choices

If you don't intend to wait long before you try and conceive again then *condoms* (internal or external, also known as male and female condoms) would suit you best. If you are not especially concerned if you do find yourself pregnant but would like to postpone it for a while then *natural family planning* would be worth considering. If you are considering not getting pregnant for the next few months, options such as *the pill* or *contraceptive cap* would be suitable. For longer periods of avoiding pregnancy *long-acting reversible contraceptives* such as the implant or the coil would be a good choice.

You can get contraception advice from your GP (family doctor) or family planning/reproductive health clinic. They can also advise you if you are anxious about future fertility or have questions about when to get pregnant, or are emotional about having to use contraception.

There is more information about contraception options and how contraceptives work via:

> The Family Planning Association's My Contraception Tool
> www.fpa.org.uk/contraception-help/my-contraception-tool
> Planned Parenthood's All About Birth Control
> www.plannedparenthood.org/learn/birth-control

TARSHI's Did You Know? Guide to Contraception
www.tarshi.net/index.asp?pid=166

The World Health Organization's guide to contraception (available in English, Arabic, Chinese, French, Russian and Spanish)
www.who.int/en/news-room/fact-sheets/detail/family-planning-contraception

Our Bodies, Ourselves Birth Control Guide (available in English and Spanish)
www.ourbodiesourselves.org/health-topics/birth-control

When you disagree on what to do next

Some people want to try again very quickly and that can introduce tensions in relationships if one of you really wants this and the other doesn't. Talking over what you want to do is a good idea, as it may reveal the person that does not want to try is anxious about physical and emotional pain; is still recovering; feels guilty; or just isn't ready yet. Understanding why you want to wait, or why you wish to try quickly (the drive to be pregnant) may not change your positions but can leave you appreciating each other's needs. It can also highlight if there are misunderstandings. If disagreements about what you want to do is causing relationship tensions or arguments then relationship therapy can help you negotiate your choices, communicate more effectively, and rebuild your relationship if closeness and kindness are missing.

Psychosexual difficulties

Following one or more miscarriages or fertility problems, relationship difficulties and sexual problems can start or worsen. Suggestions of 'trying again' or 'keep trying' may be difficult if sex is now a chore; where desire is missing; if you are still grieving or traumatized; or if you are worried that you will never get or stay pregnant.

66 *I felt like a robot.* 99 **Darren**

66 *Sex was just another job I had to check off on my daily list.* 99 **Maddie**

66 *We kept doing it, but I didn't really care about if it felt good or even my orgasms. I just wanted a baby.* 99 **Alicia**

66 *Whenever we tried to have sex it was a reminder of what we had lost. I felt so guilty even asking to do it.* 99 **Ben**

It is very common after loss to not want to have penetrative sex (or any kind of intimacy), either due to pain, psychological problems or a lack of desire. This may return given enough time, following physical and emotional recovery, or with additional support or therapy.

Other problems include vulvodynia (vulval pain) or vaginismus (where the vagina tenses when penetration is attempted so inserting fingers, a penis or a sex toy is painful and difficult). This may be especially common if your miscarriage or stillbirth were very medicalized, if you experienced injury or infection, or if your pregnancy loss was particularly traumatic. Your body may be indicating either a fear reaction to past loss or future pregnancy.

Erection problems, particularly not being able to get or stay hard (erectile dysfunction), and ejaculatory difficulties including coming too quickly (premature ejaculation) or not being able to come at all (delayed ejaculation) are also understandable, although frustrating. Being guilty about trying again, memories of your partner in distress, trauma following loss, or fears about future fertility and pregnancy can all affect your ability to relax, enjoy sex, experience orgasm, or stop anxiety getting in the way.

If sexual problems are a barrier to trying to conceive you can get support from your GP (family doctor), a psychosexual therapist (either on the NHS or via private practice), or from the following support groups and resources:

Sexual Advice Association http://sexualadviceassociation.co.uk
British Association for Counselling and Psychotherapy www.bacp.co.uk
    (you can find therapists local to you, and specify you need someone that
    can help with psychosexual problems after loss).
London Sex and Relationships Therapy www.londonsexrelationshiptherapy.
    com, particularly if you are seeking a therapist who understands gender,
    sexual and relationship diversity (GSRD). Plus consider Rainbow
    Couch www.rainbowcouch.com, Pink Therapy http://pinktherapy.com
    and Counselling in Northumberland https://counsellinginnorthumber
    land.com
Details of therapists in other countries can be found via the European
    Association for Psychotherapy www.europsyche.org, the World Council
    for Psychotherapy www.worldpsyche.org

What intimacy can look like

Framing sex as the-thing-you-have-to-do-to-get-pregnant leaves us little space for closeness, pleasure, kindness, romance, affection or love. It overlooks how touch may be an important means of communication, regardless of whether you are having penetrative sex, especially where talking may feel very raw. You may feel lonely, rejected, blamed or undesirable if, following miscarriage, all kinds of affectionate and sensual activities cease. And it completely excludes those in relationships where you do not have penetrative sex (some same-sex couples; those with chronic vaginismus, vulvodynia, or erectile dysfunction; or where disability prevents penetration).

What intimacy can include

After loss you may be uncertain what to do sexually. You may be anxious about experiencing – or causing – pain. Tied in with this may be feelings of sadness, grief, guilt, and shame – all of which can make intimacy difficult. Thinking and talking about if you feel ready – physically and emotionally – is a good idea. As is agreeing to try and see how you feel; and stopping at any point either of you are feeling anxious, in pain or not enjoying yourself.

If you have always enjoyed having sex and experienced no difficulties you may want to carry on as before your loss. But if your sex life wasn't great before the loss or you are uncertain about it since, you can begin with this exercise.

Everything that brings you pleasure – list things you have liked before, or have always wanted to explore. Here are some ideas shared by other people to get you started:

- Kissing, touching, cuddling, massage, bathing together, hair brushing
- Sharing fantasies, talking about sex, using erotica, dressing up, acting out scenes you've imagined
- Having sex in different locations (rooms in your home, hotel rooms, outdoors, in the light or darkness)
- Masturbation and/or using sex toys – alone or with a partner (either touching them or having them watch while you touch yourself)
- Giving or getting oral sex
- Reading sex advice books and manuals to pick out favourites you already like or new pleasures to share
- Trying to find as many ways to enjoy pleasure that do not involve touching genitals; or finding different ways to have your genitals touched.

Positive words – that describe what sex might represent to you. Other people's terms include: romance, love, passion, anticipation, connection, closeness, teasing, adventure. Some of these may feel right after loss, others you may be uncertain about – perhaps because you are feeling anxious about sex being potentially painful or guilt over enjoying sex after a loss.

What does sex mean to you? – most people, when asked, assume it means 'penetrative sex' (penis, finger or sex toy in vagina), but as the previous two exercises show it can be far more than this. If penetrative sex is the activity that's causing you most anxiety (either due to erection problems, genital pain, or worries about getting pregnant again) you may opt not to have any kind of penetrative sex for a set time. For some people this means agreeing not to have any kind of sexual contact for weeks or months; for others it means avoiding penetrative sex but still enjoying other sensual pleasures, or maintaining closeness and affection via cuddles and communication.

The following resources are for you to work through by yourself or with a partner to help you identify what kind of sex might work for you now or in the future:

> *Enjoy Sex (How, When and If You Want To): A Practical and Inclusive Guide* (2017). Meg-John Barker and Justin Hancock. Icon Books.
> Plus a podcast from the authors here http://megjohnandjustin.com/tag/podcast, their easy-to-use *Make Your Own Sex Manual* http://megjohnandjustin.com/product/make-your-own-sex-manual and this guide on enjoying non-genital sex http://megjohnandjustin.com/sex/enjoy-non-genital-sex
> *Come as You Are: The Surprising New Science that Will Transform Your Sex Life* (2015). Emily Nagoski. Scribe.
> *Guide to Getting it On: Unzipped* (2017). Paul Joannides and Daerick Gross Sr. Goofy Foot Press.

How not *to act if you are not having sex*

After loss neither of you may want sex for some time for the reasons outlined above. Or it may be one of you wants sex again but the other does not. Recognizing and respecting this is important, as pressurizing someone to have sex when they do not want to is always wrong but can worsen reactions to grief or trauma. Sulking, moodiness, withdrawing affection, or making unkind comments is not going to get you any kind of consensual sex, but could build up more resentments. It is okay to masturbate on your own if your partner does not want to be intimate for a while. And if you are frustrated because you wish to get pregnant again quickly, this is more likely to happen if you give a partner space and time to recover rather than pushing for intimacy before they are physically or emotionally ready.

Removing the pressure when you want to conceive

To remove the pressure for constantly having penis in vagina sex some people opt for using DIY home self-insemination kits, or a sterile cup and turkey baster may also avoid having regular intercourse. The organisations below have information on ways to get pregnant, and advice on what to do if this doesn't happen. If you've been trying consistently to get pregnant for over 6 months (without using contraception) and you're aged over 35, and for over a year and you're aged under 35, you should see your doctor. You can get more support from:

> Fertility Network UK http://fertilitynetworkuk.org
> NHS Choices www.nhs.uk/Livewell/Fertility/Pages/Fertilityhome.aspx
> Path 2 Parenthood www.path2parenthood.org
> Fertility Matters http://fertilitymatters.ca

When you decide to stop trying

Some people know that after a particularly difficult loss, a medical diagnosis, or recurrent miscarriages, that they do not want to keep trying to conceive. Others take time to reach this point, and still more resist it for as long as possible. Even if you are told there is little or no hope, you may still want to keep trying. You may reach this point by:

- Discussing your situation with your partner
- Talking to your doctor
- Seeking specialist fertility counselling
- Seeing a therapist that can help you discuss fertility options or coming to terms with infertility and involuntary childlessness
- Exploring your options with charities and support groups

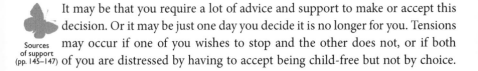

Sources of support (pp. 145–147) It may be that you require a lot of advice and support to make or accept this decision. Or it may be just one day you decide it is no longer for you. Tensions may occur if one of you wishes to stop and the other does not, or if both of you are distressed by having to accept being child-free but not by choice.

Again, therapy and support from organizations listed in Sources of support can help you navigate this difficult time; as may the communication tips suggested in Chapter 9. You may also find this leaflet from the Miscarriage Association useful: *When the Trying Stops* www.miscarriageassociation.org.uk/wp-content/uploads/2016/10/When-the-Trying-Stops.pdf

Chapter 9 (pp. 98–100)

Other options

If you know you cannot get pregnant, or have decided to stop trying, then you may continue to wish to experience intimacy (see above), but also think about other life choices. People I have worked with have considered the following. None of these are easy decisions, and many are not even choices at all but instead are a way of working within your circumstances in ways that help you best.

Child free – this may not be by choice (because you do want to be pregnant and have a baby), or by choice (as in you accept pregnancy and parenthood is not something you now wish to do)

Surrogacy – where another person carries your pregnancy for you, and you raise your child yourself

Mentoring – supporting children and young people in schools and colleges

Caring for young relatives – being an active aunt or uncle to other children in your family

Fostering – taking care of babies, children or teenagers for a short period (days or weeks) or longer term placements

Adoption – legally giving a home to a baby, child or teenager.

Too often when I have read suggestions for people struggling to get or stay pregnant I have felt frustrated with precisely the kind of advice I have offered above. If it isn't time for you to consider these options right now, you do not have to – if at all. Nevertheless all of these are options and worth considering, particularly if you are struggling to come to terms with fertility problems and want something positive to focus on. Or they can help you identify what you do – or do not – want to do.

Everyone kept saying 'you can adopt'. I didn't want to adopt! I wanted the babies I had lost. Or to have one of my own. **Isla**

Ten years after our last loss my wife suggested we become foster parents. Fifteen more years and 40-plus kids later it proved to be the best choice for us. **Malcolm**

"Our baby daughter died thirty years ago, but I have never talked to anyone about it. I didn't even tell my wife how sad I felt"

Sources of support (pp. 145–147)

Whatever happens next you may need to be flexible and adapt what you hoped to do with what is realistic; remembering there are people who can support you – that might include your doctor or other health specialists, the charities in Sources of support, faith leaders, friends, and family.

FURTHER HELP

Trying Again: A Guide to Pregnancy After Miscarriage, Stillbirth and Infant Loss (2000). Ann Douglas and John R. Sussman. Taylor Trade Press.

Tommy's Charity 'Planning for Pregnancy'
www.tommys.org/planningpregnancy

Resolve (National Infertility Association) http://resolve.org

Patient guide to infertility
https://patient.info/health/infertility-leaflet

Healthtalk Online shares discussions about infertility issues
www.healthtalk.org/peoples-experiences/pregnancy-children/
infertility/topics

Gateway Women's resources on childlessness and child-free resources
https://list.ly/list/13P-gateway-women-childless-and-child
free-resources

Gateway Women http://gateway-women.com

The Dovecote (advice and support for involuntary childlessness)
www.thedovecote.org

National Fertility Awareness Week www.nfaw.org.uk

12. Pregnant
AFTER LOSS

You may be delighted to discover you are pregnant again. But equally you may be anxious, uncertain or even fearful about the pregnancy. Getting and staying pregnant can be stressful and unnerving and that can last throughout a pregnancy, affect your birth, or even early parenthood where welcoming a new baby can coexist with mourning a loss.

If you have had one or more losses, the excitement and anticipation of past pregnancies may mean future pregnancies are not experienced with the same degree of positivity. You might be more hesitant to announce your pregnancy to other people, it may be you either see your doctor very early (due to a fear of future loss) or avoid talking to healthcare staff for as long as possible (particularly if your previous encounters with them were negative – see Chapter 4). You may be keen for key people in your life to know early so they can support you during this pregnancy and if there is another loss.

Chapter 4
(pp. 48–50)

6 *Every pregnancy has been harder to get enthusiastic about, we had several miscarriages before we had our son. It was hard to feel anything for him while he was inside me.* 9 Lucy

6 *I avoided going to see the doctor until I absolutely had to, I didn't see the point if I wasn't going to stay pregnant.* 9 D'aja

6 *We didn't tell anyone until we had had scans and even then only a few people close to us.* 9 Wei

6 *As soon as I saw the pregnancy test I asked my doctor to refer me to the Early Pregnancy Unit. I didn't believe I was pregnant, not for some while.* 9 Teuila

Common reactions to discovering you are pregnant after loss

Shock or disbelief – it may take some time for you to accept you are pregnant, particularly if you had accepted this was unlikely to happen or if you were not actively trying to conceive. For some people it is only when they have scans or develop symptoms, or even during labour they accept they are pregnant. For others it might even be a shock once their baby is born, they may continue to marvel they are a parent or struggle to accept this (see below).

Joy – being thrilled about a pregnancy, excited and full of hopes and dreams.

Superstitious – you may be anxious about tempting fate by being too happy, talking about your pregnancy openly, or even preparing for pregnancy and parenthood. You may be worried about signs and symptoms that could indicate another loss. Or have a range of activities, habits or rituals you engage in to help you feel in control or try and make your pregnancy last.

Avoiding/mistrusting healthcare – if you had poor treatment with your past pregnancy loss, or even if care was good but you now associated it with past grief and trauma you may either put off seeing your doctor, or when you are seeing doctors or midwives you do not fully open up to them, or believe what they tell you.

'Knicker checking' – being able to relax and enjoy pregnancy may be difficult, and you may be highly anxious about another loss. That might manifest itself in checking your underwear whenever you go to the bathroom for traces of blood; or worrying about any twinges or symptoms (or the lack of them).

Guilt and sadness – this may be over baby you lost, or if you've made friends through pregnancy support groups or connecting over shared experiences feel bad if you're pregnant and they are not.

Conflicted emotions – you may be pleased about being pregnant, but sad about past losses. You may feel more focused on the baby you lost rather than one you are carrying and that may trouble you. Or wish you were still pregnant with your other baby rather than this one.

Problems bonding with your bump – if you are anxious about losing another baby you might feel there is little point in connecting with your current pregnancy, or simply feel so numb that you are unable to let yourself connect.

Chapter 5
(pp. 57–58)

Stress symptoms – including struggling to sleep, relax, eat or take care of yourself. Fears of getting or staying pregnant may exacerbate existing mental health problems (especially anxiety, depression or PTSD – see Chapter 5).

How to cope if your pregnancy ends in another loss

Chapter 2
(pp. 11–12)

Chapter 6
(pp. 62–65)

Chapter 11
(p. 118)

You may feel differently from previous losses, another one may be easier or far harder (see Chapters 2 and 5). You might be better prepared (see checklist in Chapter 2) and know what to expect and be better able to navigate through healthcare (see Chapters 3 and 4). But you may also feel like you're alone, ill wished, cursed or somehow undeserving (see Chapters 5 and 6). You may be particularly anxious if you used artificial insemination and do not have the options to try this again, or only have a budget to attempt a limited attempt. If you have had a stillbirth or late miscarriage or recurrent miscarriages may want to have further investigations to identify why loss happened (see Chapter 6) and/or speak to your family doctor if you have concerns about your fertility (see Chapter 11).

If you do not want to be pregnant

While you may have wanted your previous pregnancy, it may be you decide you do not want to be pregnant again. This may be because you have not yet recovered from your past loss, due to fears over being pregnant again, relationship breakdown, or because a problem is detected with the pregnancy. In this case you may opt to terminate the pregnancy, which may be an easy or difficult decision to make. More information on your options can be found via:

British Pregnancy Advisory Service www.bpas.org
Planned Parenthood www.plannedparenthood.org
Marie Stopes International www.mariestopes.org
International Planned Parenthood Federation www.ippf.org

These organizations also offer contraception advice and information about pregnancy, and wider women's health services.

If you stay pregnant

You should alert your GP and midwife about previous pregnancy losses, even if you did not seek medical help for them at the time.

Tell healthcare providers if you are still distressed by your previous miscarriage(s) or are very concerned about your current pregnancy. You might want to write this down if it is difficult to speak openly, or ask a friend or partner to come with you to help you feel more confident or explain if you feel unable.

If you are at risk of further miscarriages your doctor can advise on further tests to establish what might be causing pregnancy loss, they may also recommend additional treatment and counselling. It may be that in the case of high-risk pregnancies you will need regular monitoring in hospital or a hospital admission.

You may be more anxious before your birth, particularly if your previous pregnancy loss(es) were very painful, or if you went through labour. Discussing your birth options with a midwife may be reassuring. Including in your birth plan that you had a past loss and are anxious about delivery and what you need in way of support (there are templates for birth plans available online, such as this example from the NHS: www.nhs.uk/conditions/pregnancy-and-baby/how-to-make-birth-plan – you can adapt this to suit your needs depending on where you are located and what information about past losses you wish healthcare staff to know). If you had a particularly traumatic loss previously including bleeding, clotting, an emergency delivery, late loss or stillbirth, then you may want to prepare with a midwife before birth – the Birth Trauma Association www.birthtraumaassociation.org.uk may also have information to help.

If you are constantly crying, distracted, detached, irritable, disconnected from your pregnancy, feeling low or suicidal you may be experiencing prenatal depression. This can happen even if you wanted to be pregnant very much (I certainly experienced it with my last pregnancy), and may initially be confused by you being upset over a past loss. If you or those close to you notice you have these symptoms then speak to your GP or midwife. The charity PANDAS has useful advice about recognizing prenatal depression and treatment options www.pandasfoundation.org.uk/prenatal-depression and you can also get support from:

APNI (Association for Postnatal Illness) https://apni.org
Perinatal Anxiety and Depression Australia (PANDA) www.panda.org.au
Postpartum Support International www.postpartum.net

Ways to enjoy a healthy pregnancy

While there are no guarantees that future pregnancies may end in loss, there are some things you can do to reduce your chances of pregnancy loss and enjoy a healthy pregnancy.

- As soon as you want to try again, or ideally 3 months prior to trying to conceive, take folic acid tablets daily
- Stop smoking
- Reduce or cut out alcohol
- Cut out caffeine
- Ensure you are a healthy weight (not over- or underweight)
- Eat a healthy, balanced diet
- Sleep on your side
- Seek health advice from your doctor if you have a pre-existing physical or mental health condition
- Check your vaccinations are up to date
- Avoid unpasteurized milk, cheese and meat pâtés
- Wash fruit and vegetables thoroughly before eating
- Get checked for undiagnosed or symptomless STIs
- Wash your hands after going to the toilet and before preparing meals
- Avoid travel to countries in malaria zones (or, if you live in one, use bed nets and take anti-malarials as directed by your doctor).
- Avoid contact with sheep and goats
- If you have a cat use gloves when cleaning out the litter tray (or have someone do this job for you while you are pregnant)

What you may be worried about

Will sex hurt the baby/cause a miscarriage?

Unless you have been otherwise recommended to avoid sex by your doctor, then penetrative sexual activities and orgasm are not going to cause a miscarriage nor hurt your baby. As your pregnancy progresses you may need to change the positions you have sex in so you can feel comfortable and supported, and while your baby will be able to hear your breathing and your heartbeat and feel you moving it will not know you are having sex nor be harmed by it. If you want to enjoy intimacy during your pregnancy you can, and there is more information in Chapter 11 about ways to explore pleasure.

Chapter 11
(pp. 116–117)

What might increase my risk of miscarriage?

Going to work, exercise or being busy may be sources of worry to you. In general if your pregnancy is healthy then everyday life should continue. However, if you are struggling to cope mentally or physically; if you have other painful pregnancy symptoms or mobility problems; or if you are worried that you could be at risk of pregnancy loss then you may want to talk to your boss, HR department, gym manager/personal trainer, and doctor as appropriate.

Did I not love the baby I lost enough?

One of the strange, superstitious beliefs (see above) that can come with a pregnancy and newborn is a worry that you somehow caused previous pregnancy loss because you did not care enough about your baby, or that in loving the one you currently have you are somehow disloyal. Or that because you are not as excited about this pregnancy that you are liable to bring on a loss. None of this is true. You cannot stay pregnant based on love nor how much you want a baby. You did not cause a miscarriage or stillbirth by how you felt and whether you are very connected or not to your new pregnancy or baby, it does not mean you care more or less about them or a past loss – nor indicate anything about your ability to be a good parent.

Early parenthood

Having a baby may be overwhelming and busy, it may mean for some time you do not focus on past losses, which may be something you are later glad of, or can feel guilty about. You may find yourself grieving for the baby you lost, along with loving the one you now have. Or you may feel connected to past losses by having a newborn.

If your past losses were traumatic, and if you had struggled during your pregnancy or birth, you may find bonding with your baby is difficult. Moreso if you had any complications arising from your birth or if your baby was premature or has any health conditions. Accepting support and care here is important, as is noting some of your current reactions may be based on past losses.

You may be overly anxious or protective of your baby, not feeling confident about their development, or your abilities to parent. You might be worried about leaving them alone to sleep or in the care of other people, or just feel generally stressed about having a new baby. Talking to your health visitor, midwife or trusted friends and family that have children, along with taking parenting classes may reassure you.

It is also not unusual to experience postnatal depression (PND) even if you really wanted to be pregnant (and after previous losses; I had this with my youngest son). The symptoms of this include:

- Consistently feeling sad or low
- Not being interested in what's going on around you (including existing children), or in things you previously enjoyed
- Feeling tired or exhausted all the time
- Insomnia during the night, and sleepiness in the day
- Feeling like you cannot look after your baby (either lacking confidence to do so, or not having the energy or interest)
- Overeating or avoiding food
- Not being able to bond with or be close to your baby
- Feeling overly anxious about your baby
- Struggling to focus, make decisions or concentrate
- Thoughts about self-harm or suicide
- Feelings of agitation, anxiety, irritability or lethargy
- Scary and intrusive thoughts – either of hurting your baby or your baby being hurt
- Feeling disassociated from the world around you
- Believing your family would be better off if you were not around

If you or a partner notices one or more of these symptoms you should speak to your midwife, health visitor or doctor.

General ways to help you cope

Chapter 8 (pp. 88–93) Through your pregnancy and early parenthood you may want to try the suggestions for self-care in Chapter 8.

Pregnancy support groups and parenting classes may help you feel more confident, and also be a place to meet other people in similar positions or ask for support if you need it.

Sources of support (pp. 145–147) While the organizations listed in Sources of support are primarily focused on miscarriage and stillbirth, they can still provide comfort and reassurance if you are pregnant after loss and during new parenthood.

You may not feel like doing much to mark your pregnancy or early parenthood, but later may regret this. Doing things like photographing yourself during pregnancy, noting pregnancy and new baby milestones in a diary, or finding ways to celebrate different stages of your pregnancy and early parenthood may be something you enjoy later. Or perhaps allow other family members or friends to be part of it. If you feel you cannot celebrate or be part of things, talk to your doctor about ante or postnatal depression (see above), and do not be harsh on yourself. There will be opportunities to make memories with your child in the future.

FURTHER HELP

Sidelines (High Risk Pregnancy Support) www.sidelines.org

Kicks Count www.kickscount.org.uk

Project Alive and Kicking www.projectaliveandkicking.org

National Childbirth Trust www.nct.org.uk

Rainbow Antenatal (support for pregnancies after loss) www.rainbowantenatal.com

Dear Orla (provides downloadable, printable stickers to put on maternity notes and alert practitioners you are pregnant after loss) https://dear-orla.com

Lullaby Trust www.lullabytrust.org.uk

Trying Again: A Guide to Pregnancy After Miscarriage, Stillbirth and Infant Loss (2000). Ann Douglas and John R. Sussman. Taylor Trade Publishing.

Pregnancy After a Loss: A Guide to Pregnancy After a Miscarriage, Stillbirth or Infant Death (1999). Carol Cirulli. Lanham Berkley Books.

Celebrating Pregnancy Again: Restoring the Lost Joys of Pregnancy After the Loss of a Child (2013). Franchesca Cox. Create Space Independent Publishing Platform.

Joy at the End of the Rainbow: A Guide to Pregnancy After Loss (2017). Amanda Ross-White.

Expecting Sunshine: A Journey of Grief, Healing and Pregnancy After Loss (2017). She Writes Press.

The Miscarriage Association www.miscarriageassociation.org.uk/your-feelings/pregnancyafter miscarriage

PRE AND POSTNATAL DEPRESSION

Cognitive Behavioural Therapy for Perinatal Distress (2014). Amy Wenzel. Routledge.

Royal College of Psychiatrists Guide to Post Natal Depression www.rcpsych.ac.uk/mentalhealthinfoforall/problems/postnatal mentalhealth/postnataldepression.aspx

PANDAS www.pandasfoundation.org.uk

Association for Postnatal Illness https://apni.org

Postnatal Illness www.pni.org.uk

Mental Health Guide for First Nations, Metis and Inuit People www.wrha.mb.ca/aboriginalhealth/services/files/ MentalHealthGuide.pdf

13. Remembering

This chapter shares approaches myself and others have found useful when marking and moving forward after loss.

Memorials can be a means of remembering your loss(es), celebrating a pregnancy even if it did not go to term. Thinking about and remembering miscarriage can be very healing, but if it is something that distresses you and it is easier to cope by not dwelling on your losses that is fine too.

There is no right or wrong way to remember a loss. You should not feel uncomfortable if you still wish to do this years after the event. Or if you find over time you no longer wish to do so. It does not mean you are bad, uncaring or disloyal if you do not wish to remember. Or that you are crazy because you never want to forget. If you are finding months or years on you are still struggling to cope with daily life because you are distressed, you can talk to your doctor.

Ways of remembering

If you do want to mark your loss you may want to pick something personal and meaningful to you and your partner. That might include:

Giving your baby a name – you may have already decided upon a name for your baby prior to your loss (this is particularly common if you have been trying for some time to get pregnant and/or using assisted conception). Or afterwards you may want to consider a name both to comfort yourself, recognize your baby, for a death certificate (if appropriate), or funeral arrangements. Some people pick a family name, or descriptors like angel or butterfly.

Jewellery – this might include a necklace, bracelet, or ring. A token you can wear and keep close may feel comforting. This can be purchased from jewelers or antique shops, although specialist stockists are increasingly popular – some include engraving to include names or key dates (search online for 'memorial' or 'remembrance' jewellery). Or you may want to make your own.

Trees, plants and gardens – buying a long-lasting plant, planting a tree in your own garden or having one named in a woodland. Or dedicating an area of your garden to wildflowers or attractive plants that attract bees, birds, bats and butterflies.

Tattoos – are a more permanent reminder that could represent your loss through an image, or where names and dates of your babies and losses are recorded. As with jewellery this is something you can carry with you for always.

Art and ornaments – pictures that feel calming and you feel particularly drawn to may be something to display at home or work. Some people prefer ornaments, vases or other keepsakes to display.

Photographs – if you experienced a late loss or stillbirth you may be offered the opportunity to have a photograph taken with your baby. While not everyone wants to do this, it can be an important reminder. Groups offering this service (where a photographer will photograph you and your baby for free) include:

Remember My Baby (UK) www.remembermybaby.org.uk
Now I Lay Me Down To Sleep (US and worldwide)
   www.nowilayme downtosleep.org

As well as offering services for families, these organizations plus Gifts of Remembrance (UK) http://giftsofremembrance.co.uk also train photographers to work sensitively with parents who have recently experienced loss. Alternatively, you may want to photograph your baby yourself – your midwives should help make this an empowering experience for you.

Following recovery after miscarriage, some people feel they wish to help other bereaved families so offer services like photography, or creating comfort/memory boxes for people to take home from hospital after a late loss or still-birth. These typically include a candle, teddy or small stuffed toy, an inspirational poem, an uplifting book, or other keepsake.

Other keepsakes – if you had a stillbirth you might also want to take a footprint, keep your baby's clothing or blanket; a lock of hair; identification bracelet; details of your baby's weight, length and other physical measurements; hospital records; or a print out of your baby's heartbeat.

Baby items – you may have already bought items of clothing; nappies, bottles, a cot, toys, and other baby essentials you decide to keep as mementoes. However, if it is impractical or too painful to keep these, you may want to gift them to another family or charity. Or you might hold on to them if you are hoping to have another baby in the future.

Involving others – you may want relatives or existing children to join with some of the suggestions in this chapter, or creating their own meaningful events. Families have created artwork, letters to their lost baby, or poems to note their feelings.

Scrapbooks – you may have scan photos, pictures of you during your pregnancy, or photos of your baby you wish to put into a scrapbook. Perhaps with other meaningful poems or quotes; a naming certificate, letters of condolence or messages from friends and family; newspaper announcements about your loss; pressed flowers from a funeral bouquet; a copy of the memorial order of service; or other relevant keepsakes. Some people prefer to create a 'memory box' they decorate or purchase to keep precious reminders in.

Online memories – Alongside creating, planting and crafting ideas outlined above, nowadays people also choose to remember their losses online. This can include joining websites or support groups where you document your stories, or create virtual memorials. For example

> The Miscarriage Association's Stars of Remembrance
> www.miscarriageassociation.org.uk/your-feelings/marking-your-loss/
> stars-of-remembrance
> Remembered Forever www.remembered-forever.co.uk
> Gone Too Soon www.gonetoosoon.org
> Stillbirthday (allows you to celebrate your baby's birthday)
> https://stillbirthday.com
> Caring Bridge (lets you update your health news so you don't have to keep telling people what is going on) www.caringbridge.org
> Searching for 'light a virtual candle' online brings up faith and secular groups offering this service. Some people find blogging helps them document a loss (and inform other people about miscarriage), while others use social media to remember. (Note some social media sites save your memories and share them years later. If this is liable to be upsetting for you then it may be sensible to delete discussions about loss once you have benefited from them.)

Crafting – knitting, sewing or embroidery may all be ways to either mark your own loss, or help others. In support groups I've attended people have talked about creating patchwork to both occupy their mind and focus their loss. Others have extended this to community crafting – you can find out more from the Craftivist Collective www.craftivist-collective.com or supporting organizations that need knitted items – including blankets, sweaters/jumpers, hats and scarves, soft toys, or prosthetic breasts for cancer survivors. Some of these are created for children's charities which may be too painful to connect with, while other people find making clothing, toys or blankets for babies (including stillborn babies) leaves them feeling like they are doing something important and useful. Organizations who need your creative skills include:

SANDS have knitting and crochet patterns for their memory boxes www.uk-sands.org/get-involved/volunteer-sands/knit-sands

Knitted Knockers (for breast cancer survivors) www.knittedknockers.org

BLISS patterns for toys and clothing for preemie babies www.bliss.org.uk/knit-for-premature-babies (you can also search for 'preemie knitting patterns' and find free ones online, and your neonatal unit can advise on what they want).

Woolly Hugs are a network of knitters creating a variety of items for different causes. These can be found here www.woollyhugs.org/ongoing-projects and you may be particularly interested in supporting Angel Hugs and Angel Bears (see link for details).

Similar organizations include Knit for Life www.knitforlife.co.uk

Warm Up America! www.warmupamerica.org

Afghans for Afghans www.afghansforafghans.org

Binky Patrol https://binkypatrol.org

Mother Bear Project www.motherbearproject.org

Speaking out and sharing stories – Hearing from other people in the same position as you can be hugely powerful. Sharing your experiences on an online support group, for example, might be initially done to help you cope but ends up informing other people too. You may want to do this more formally by helping at support groups, moderating local social media pages for people affected by babyloss, or offering to give talks to healthcare staff or therapists based on your experiences. Some people use their losses to campaign for better awareness and care. You can find these stories or enquire about donating yours through the charities listed in Sources of support; or via the Experience Project www.experienceproject.com

Sources of support
(pp. 145–147)

Events for you to join

Hospitals and charities often organize annual multi-faith and secular memorial services specifically designed for people that have experienced miscarriage, stillbirth and infant loss. You may find attending these helps you feel able to more formally mark your loss, and to connect with others who have been through similar experiences. Most hospitals also have a book of remembrance where you can write down the date of your loss and name of your baby.

If you are religious your faith leader will have specific blessings, prayers or services that can be offered immediately after a loss, and there may be services you can attend at your place of worship to remember and connect with other people in similar situations who have also lost a baby and share the same beliefs as you. Some people also find home visits and spiritual comfort from faith leaders or the wider religious community reassuring and practical – for example people offering food or help with shopping if you need it.

Babyloss Awareness Week runs from 9–15 October every year and includes events, services, meetings, fundraising, education, and outreach. It always ends with a 'wave of light' celebration where people light candles on the evening of the 15th at 7pm (their time). People also share photos, stories, poems, and details about the babies they have lost, particularly on social media. In some towns and cities key buildings and bridges are lit up with pink and blue to mark the occasion and this may coincide with other community memorial events. Charities across the world join this initiative and there is more information about it via the Babyloss Awareness Week website https://babyloss-awareness.org

Lights of Love services are held annually in December, with carols, readings, and music
www.uk-sands.org/support-you/remembering-your-baby/lights-love

Children's Grief Awareness Week www.childrensgriefawarenessweek.com happens in the second week in November and offers support and the opportunity to grieve for siblings or other children in your family affected by loss.

World Childless Week worldchildlessweek.net runs in the second week in September, raising awareness of issues faced by the childless not by choice (cnbc) community.

Sources of support (pp. 145–147) If there are no events local to you, or you are unsure of where you may get support to remember, the charities listed in Sources of support can advise. Or you may want to establish an event of your own.

Certificates

Depending on when you lost your pregnancy you may be offered a death certificate for your baby. Some people find this difficult to accept as it makes their loss feel more real, others are comforted by noting their baby is officially documented. Certification policies vary depending on country and state law, but are usually given to late miscarriage and stillbirth. However, in some hospitals, midwives can provide certificates for you to mark your loss if you had an early miscarriage, or ectopic pregnancy. You could also create your own certificate noting the date of your loss, your babies name (if you have one), and any other memorable information. The Miscarriage Association's guidance for professionals can also be adapted to suit your needs www.miscarriageassociation.org.uk/information/for-health-professionals/certification.

Alternatively you may not want any kind of certificate, and if that is your preference it should be dealt with tactfully. If for official purposes a death certificate is issued, it may be another friend or family member can look after it for you if it is too upsetting for you to keep.

Funerals and memorial services

An official marking of a loss can be healing and powerful, as may gathering friends and family together to witness your baby's passing. You can organize this via your faith leader, or if you are not religious you can discuss with a funeral service or the charities listed in Sources of support what your options are for a secular service.

Sources
of support
(pp. 145–147)

If you wish to have a cremation or burial this should be accommodated regardless of when your loss occurred. If you are unable to have a burial or cremation you can still have a memorial service or other gathering to mark your loss. This may happen in your place of worship, at home, or in a place of beauty or significance to you and your wider family.

Organizing a funeral may be difficult if you are still healing physically and psychologically after loss. Funeral homes are sympathetic to this and your hospital or bereavement midwife can also help if you are unsure where to begin making funeral arrangements. It may be you wish to be actively involved in planning every aspect of the funeral, or prefer to let trusted friends or loved ones undertake this if you feel unable or are too unwell. They can clarify plans with you so you still feel included and have the funeral you want for your baby.

Asking about the cost of funeral and funeral options is important. In some locations burial and cremation fees are waived for babies and children but there may be other costs you would not anticipate. Asking for advice about what is expected and seeking financial assistance if appropriate is a good idea, you should be able to remember your baby regardless of your income. There is more information for you and the professionals you are being supported by via:

Child Funeral Charity www.childfuneralcharity.org.uk
Children are Butterflies www.childrenarebutterflies.org.uk/assistance
SANDS booklet: *Deciding About a Funeral for Your Baby*
    www.sands.org.uk/support/bereavement-support/deciding-about-
    funeral-your-baby

If your baby needs transporting from the hospital to the mortuary or funeral home you should check how this is managed and if it incurs any additional costs.

For a burial or cremation you should expect to pick a funeral casket (which may be open or closed), and what your baby will wear or be wrapped in. You can use a home-made shawl, blanket, or outfit, or can buy funeral clothing for babies via:

Heavenly Angels in Need www.heavenlyangelsinneed.com
A Child of Mine www.achildofmine.org.uk/Baby-Burial-Clothing/I120.htm
Something Precious https://baby-burial-gowns.co.uk
Jacqui's Preemie Pride burial clothing
    www.jacquispreemiepride.com/collections

Other things to consider are whether you would like flowers, donations made to a charity of your choice (e.g. some of the organizations listed throughout this book or in Sources of support, or the hospital where your pregnancy loss happened). Along with invitations to the funeral or memorial service and an order of service (which may include a photograph of your baby or an image that reminds you of them).

Sources of support (pp. 145–147)

If you have a burial or cremation you will have the opportunity to spend a short time with your baby prior to the funeral service beginning. Some people find this difficult and opt not to do it, while others find it a useful way of marking a final farewell.

In the service you may want to say a prayer, give a short reading, share a poem, talk together about how you feel, sing songs or hymns, dance together, or sit in supportive silence. Appendix B in *A Silent Sorrow. Pregnancy Loss: Guidance and Support for You and Your Family (2nd edn)* by Ingrid Kohn and Perry-Lynn Moffitt (Routledge, 2000) has a number of selected readings for all faiths and none you may wish to include, and if you are religious then Chapter 10 of the same text – *Finding Solace in Your Religion* – may be meaningful.

Helping others as a way of marking a loss

After a loss, some people feel like they want to help others in the same situation, particularly if the care they have been given was either very good (so they wish to give something back in return), or very poor (where they want to ensure nobody else goes through something similar). I didn't feel this way immediately after any of my losses, but latterly I felt, as many do, that I wanted to do *something*. For me that something ended up as doing research, collecting and sharing other people's stories, and writing this book. You may have a similar desire to make a difference as a means of remembering or helping.

You can do this through joining existing support groups, offering advice online or in person, establishing or assisting with local drop-in services for people affected by miscarriage and stillbirth, blogging or Instagramming about loss, or fundraising for charities and hospitals offering pregnancy loss advice and care; participating in research studies about pregnancy loss; or running marathons, hosting cake sales, quiz nights or other events.

This may be a long-term part of your identity, or just for a short period. It is okay to stop activities if they are no longer helping; if they are making you feel worse; or, more positively, you feel you have moved on.

When you were unable to remember as you wanted

Sometimes miscarriages happen when you are on the toilet and you flush either without thinking or because you do not know what else to do. In such cases you may feel upset and guilty, and people have said to me *I did not get to say goodbye, I didn't give the baby a proper send off, I failed them*. You may also feel separated from your baby if you had a medical or surgical management of miscarriage in hospital – *I couldn't stop worrying about how I'd left her there*. Noting this was not your fault and nor have you failed is important, but creating memorials in such cases may be especially powerful and reassuring. You did not have a choice about your pregnancy ending, but you do have full control over how you wish to remember your losses.

You may find you and your partner, friends or family want to remember in different ways. It is fine to allow each other space to memorialize in ways that help you best. It isn't a competition. It is okay to say to some family members who wish to make a gesture that if it makes them happy you are fine with it, but if you do not want to be party to it you can make that clear also. If you or your partner does not want to mark the loss but the other one does it is not an indication they are being unreasonable or that you are unfeeling. But you may need to find ways to compromise so that you can feel comfortable in marking – or not marking – your loss(es).

If your family is particularly difficult or overbearing, try and take over any memorial plans you have, or make your loss all about them, then you may be pushed into remembering in ways you do not want or feel excluded from. This can be cruel and traumatic. Being assertive about what you want is important, but if that is not possible you may find other suggestions in this chapter healing as you can pick something privately that is *your* way to remember your baby.

If you think you're remembering in unusual ways

Grieving and remembering is something that we all do in diverse ways and to different degrees, so you might find yourself doing something out of the norm – talking to your baby; imagining how they might have been; daydreaming about them as if they are growing with you; or accepting you are really not that upset and do not wish that to change. All of these happen – even if we don't talk about it openly.

Forgetting

Losses may be fixed in your memory or noted in your diary, but for some people if there are a number of losses; if you were unsure about being pregnant or miscarrying; if your losses happened a long time ago; or if you were unable to mark them at the time, it may be difficult to note exactly when a loss happened. And trauma may mean people shut out the specifics. If you cannot remember key dates or events or feel your memories are fading you might feel a sense of relief. It may not trouble you. But if you feel the desire to remember the ideas in this chapter can help.

Love continues after loss

Love is a powerful emotion and one woman in a support group I attended reminded us '*love means you have never abandoned your baby*'. There are plenty of expensive ways to remember a loss, and lots you can create yourself at low cost. But the basic act of love, remembrance, and care can never be underestimated, nor lost.

FURTHER HELP

Healing Your Grieving Heart After Stillbirth (2013). Alan D. Wolfelt and Raelynn Maloney. Companion Books – this text is useful for any kind of loss, and has numerous suggestions you may want to try written in a friendly and compassionate tone. You may find 'The Mourners Code' at the end of the book particularly empowering.

Loved Baby: 13 Devotions Helping you Grieve and Cherish Your Child After Pregnancy Loss (2017). Sarah Philpott. Broadstreet Publishing Group.

May We All Heal: Playbook For Creative Healing After Loss (2016). Nathalie Himmelrich and Kerstin Poth. Reach for the Sky.

AFFIRMATIONS DURING AND AFTER LOSS

I am not alone

I can cope

This may be difficult, but I will get through it

I can express my feelings however suits me best

I can try again tomorrow

I can choose if and how to remember

If I have questions I can find answers

If I need support there is help out there for me

I am NOT alone.

Sources of
SUPPORT

The following organizations offer information and support for you during and after pregnancy loss. You can use them whenever your loss occurred; and they are available to help whether you had one loss, or many; and include support for partners, and advice for different faiths.

These organizations offer a variety of helplines, email advice, support groups on social media, and information booklets and resources on their websites. In addition, many offer local branches that host meetings and fundraising events where you can connect with other people who have been through similar experiences.

If there are no resources in your country you may find those listed below still can be helpful, although they may need adapting to meet your specific local needs. Some of the organizations listed below offer advice in multiple languages alongside English.

Miscarriage (early and late)

Miscarriage Association www.miscarriageassociation.org.uk
The Miscarriage Manual http://inciid.org/miscarriage-manual
March of Dimes Miscarriage Guide
 www.marchofdimes.org/complications/miscarriage.aspx
Miscarriage (Reddit's miscarriage conversations)
 www.reddit.com/r/Miscarriage

Antenatal testing

Antenatal Results and Choices www.arc-uk.org
A Heartbreaking Choice www.aheartbreakingchoice.com
Contact A Family https://contact.org.uk

Ectopic pregnancy

Ectopic Pregnancy Trust www.ectopic.org.uk
March of Dimes' Ectopic Pregnancy Guide
 www.marchofdimes.org/complications/ectopic-pregnancy.aspx

Miscarriage Association's Ectopic Pregnancy Guide
www.miscarriageassociation.org.uk/information/ectopic-pregnancy

Molar Pregnancy

Molar pregnancy support and information http://molarpregnancy.co.uk
Miscarriage Association's Molar Pregnancy Guide
www.miscarriageassociation.org.uk/information/molar-pregnancy

Premature delivery and pre-eclampsia

Action on Pre-Eclampsia https://action-on-pre-eclampsia.org.uk
Little Heartbeats (preterm prelabour rupture of membranes)
www.little-heartbeats.org.uk

Stillbirth

SANDS www.uk-sands.org
Babyloss www.babyloss.com
Aching Arms http://achingarms.co.uk
Towards Tomorrow Together www.towards-tomorrow.com
Hope After Loss www.hopeafterloss.org
Something Precious (small baby burial clothes) https://baby-burial-gowns.co.uk
HAND (Help After Neonatal Death) www.handonline.org
Mommies Enduring Neonatal Death (MEND) www.mend.org
Norwegian SIDS and Stillbirth Society www.lub.no
Still Project http://stillproject.org
Star Legacy Foundation http://starlegacyfoundation.org
March of Dimes' Stillbirth Guide
www.marchofdimes.org/complications/stillbirth.aspx
International Stillbirth Alliance http://stillbirthalliance.org
Stillbirth Stories http://stillbirthstories.org
Return to Zero: HOPE http://rtzhope.org
Life After Loss www.lifeafterloss.org.uk
Beyond Bea www.beyondbea.co.uk

All baby loss (miscarriage, ectopic pregnancy, and stillbirth support)

ThePinksnBlues www.thepinksnblues.co.uk
Tommy's www.tommys.org/our-The Pink Elephants Support Network
https://pinkelephantssupport.com
Centre for Loss in Multiple Births (CLIMB) www.climb-support.org

The Pink Elephants Support Network https://pinkelephantssupport.com
Infants Remembered in Silence (IRIS) www.irisremembers.com
MISS Foundation https://missfoundation.org
A place to remember www.aplacetoremember.com
AMEND (Aiding Mothers and Fathers Experiencing Neonatal Death)
www.amendgroup.com
Babies Remembered www.wintergreenpress.org
Love and Loss Project http://lovelossproject.com
Saying Goodbye www.sayinggoodbye.org
A Bed for My heart https://abedformyheart.com
Child Death Families Finland http://kapy.fi
SHARE Pregnancy and Infant Loss Support http://nationalshare.org
Petals Charity http://petalscharity.org

Maternity, rights, and justice

White Ribbon Alliance www.whiteribbonalliance.org
Black Mamas Matter Alliance https://blackmamasmatter.org
National Bereavement Care Pathway www.nbcpathway.org.uk
Jhpiego www.jhpiego.org

Infertility and childlessness

Gateway Women www.gateway-women.com
Still Standing (Child loss and infertility) http://stillstandingmag.com
Missing GRACE Organisation www.missinggrace.org
Silent Sorority http://silentsorority.com
Walk In Our Shoes https://walkinourshoes.net
Fertility Network UK http://fertilitynetwork.org

Pregnant after loss

Pregnancy After Loss https://pregnancyafterlosssupport.com
Subsequent Pregnancy After Loss (SPALS) http://spals.com
Miscarriage Association's Pregnant After Miscarriage
www.miscarriageassociation.org.uk/your-feelings/pregnancyaftermiscarriage

Social media chats

Alongside support groups on social media, there are a number of dedicated
pregnancy loss and related mental health chats that happen on Twitter. These
are open to anyone and you can either read what is shared, or join in if you

wish. You can find the conversations by using the hashtags below. All chats start at 8pm (GMT) and last one hour.

#PANDAShr and #childlesshour are on Sundays
#FastLossChat is on Mondays
#BabyLossHour is on Tuesdays
#PNDHour is on Wednesdays

Hashtags

If you are looking for information about pregnancy loss on social media, e.g. Facebook, Instagram, Twitter, blogs, or wish to raise awareness or share your story, the following hashtags will connect you with other people interested in specific baby loss topics. They cover pregnancy loss and wider issues around fertility, mental health, and diversity and you can mix and match to find or convey your particular needs. (While people generally use lowercase letters for their hashtags, if you want to reach a wider audience who might be using screen readers, starting every new word in a hashtag with a capital letter is a good idea. For example #pregnancyloss would be better written as #PregnancyLoss.)

Pregnancy loss

#pregnancyloss #miscarriage #babyloss #babylosssupport #BlightedOvum #latemiscarriage #lateloss #LossExp #pregnancyandinfantloss #pails #pailsparent #ectopic #ectopicpregnancy #ectopicsupport #SIDS #stillborn #stillbirth #stillborn #infantloss #infantlosssupport #childloss #neonataldeath #NBCP

Bereavement and remembering

#butterfly #stillloved #remembermybaby #angelbaby #grief #loss #love #notforgotten #rememberedforever #baby #wrappedinourhearts #emptyarms #achingarms #stilllovingyou

Parents

#angelmommy #angelmummy #angeldaddy #daddytoanangel #motherhood #fatherhood #bereavedmother #bereavedparent #bereavedfather #grievingparents #mothersday #fathersday #dadsgrievetoo #dadsmatter #partnerstoo

LGBT

#lesbianmom #lesbianmummy #bimom #bimummy #2mommies #twomommies #twomummies #samelove #loveislove #queer #rainbowfamily #lgbtqia #lgbtsupport #LGBTPregnancyLoss #LGBTMiscarriage #Trans #Transgender

Fertility and assisted conception

#IVF #ivfjourney #iui #iuijourney #ttc #ttcjourney #ttccommunity #ttcsisters #ttcbrothers #ttcfamily #pcos #endometriosis #clomid #ovulation #womb #wombhealth

Termination for medical reasons

#TMFR #TOP #Termination #Abortion

Surrogacy and Adoption

#donorbaby #surrogacy #fostering #adoption

Pregnant after loss

#pregnancy #pregnantafterloss #pgs #parentingafterloss #keepongrowingbaby #rainbowbaby #MatExp

Young parents

#TeenMom #TeenMum #TeenDad #YoungParent #YoungAndPregnant #YoungAndMiscarried

Infertility and childlessness

#childfree #childless #nochild #involuntarychildlessness #nobaby #nobabies #babyless #marriednokids #infertility #infertilitysucks #thisiswhatinfertilitylookslike #unexplainedinfertility #childlessness

Mental health

#mentalhealth #anxiety #depression #depressionanxiety #anxietydepression #PTSD #trauma #madpride #bpd #bipolar #ocd #schizophrenia #schizotribe

Postnatal depression

#pnd #pndhour

Black, Indigenous, and People of Colour

#BIPOC #blackwomen #blackwoman #blackwomenshealth #blacksisters #blackgirlmagic #blacklivesmatter #latina #latinx #latino #hispanic #mexican #indigenous #native #nativepride #firstnations

Disability and chronic illness

#disabled #disability #criplife #actuallyautistic #asd #hasautism #actuallyautistic #thebarriersweface #everydayableism #disabodyposi #deaf #blind #deafblind #invisibleillness #chronicillness #chroniclife #spoonie

Awareness and activism

#breakingthesilence #saytheirname #miscourage #Ihadamiscarriage #miscarriageawareness #babylossawareness #Iam1in4 #Iam1in5 #1in4 #1in5 #waveoflight #weremember #miscarriagesucks #miscarriagematters #youarenotalone #bethelight

A message from Petra

I share regular news and updates about pregnancy loss, and links to other charities and organizations offering support on Twitter @flyaway_birds and positive messages of self-care on Instagram (www.instagram.com/ petraboynton). Additional updates and support materials can be found at www.copingwithpregnancyloss.com, and you can also message me through this site. All of the organizations listed above are best placed to offer you immediate help, and while I cannot provide therapy or medical advice I am always happy to hear your feedback and suggestions for other resources and materials that might help others dealing with pregnancy loss. I'm also glad to help journalists with stories on pregnancy loss, and deliver training and support to charities and health organizations who are seeking to improve their services or their research on pregnancy loss.

If you are interested in seeing the other resources and publications I used to write this book, they can be found at www.copingwithpregnancyloss.com/ bibliography.

However you came to find this book, I hope it helped you, I wish you well with your future journeys. Thank you for reading.

As well as the books, resources and websites listed in this book, you can find all the other publications and resources that were consulted here: www.routledge.com/9781138047723.

Index